Enjoy!
Merrie Sue Holton

Power & Stride

The Nancy Burggraf Story

Power & Stride

The Nancy Burggraf Story

by
Merrie Sue Holtan

ISBN: 978-1-880654-41-5

Unless otherwise noted, all images provided by the *Roseau Times Region Collection*. Roseau County Historical Society.

Designed by Angela Wix
Edited by Lindsey Cunneen

Power & Stride: The Nancy Burggraf Story
By Merrie Sue Holtan

Pogo Press
An Imprint of Finney Company
8075 215th Street West
Lakeville, Minnesota 55044
www.pogopress.com
www.finneyco.com

1 3 5 7 9 10 8 6 4 2
Printed in the United States of America

Acknowledgments

With gratitude

To my family for their patience and support.

To the family of Nancy Burggraf for sharing her story.

To professors and students in the Minnesota State University Moorhead Creative Writing program for continued feedback and consultation.

To the creative team who put together the documentary *Power & Stride*.

To the community of Roseau, hockey players, coaches, and the Roseau County Historical Society.

To Nancy Burggraf who lived a story that needs to be told.

Table of Contents

Foreword

It all began in a college speech class. The assignment: a speech of tribute to someone you admire. First year student Kari Hagen, from Roseau, Minnesota, took the podium with confidence and left it with a classroom of 24 students and me, the teacher, in tears. This was the first I had ever heard of Nancy Burggraf, the first woman nominated to the United States Hockey Hall of Fame.

"Why," asked one student in the class, "haven't we heard of her before? She should be famous."

Kari's speech and Nancy Burggraf got lost among my day-to-day duties until a few weeks later as I sat in the dental chair for an annual cleaning with my dental hygienist, Becky. With my mouth wide open, I browsed over the many articles, photos, and family memorabilia Becky had posted on her wall. And there she was, staring down at me—Nancy Burggraf. Pushing away the suction tube, I asked, "Why do you have that woman on your wall?"

"That's my mom," Becky replied.

In the days and weeks that followed, Becky Lommen, the eldest Burggraf child, and Bernie, Nancy's husband, shared Nancy's life story with me. As a freelance writer for more than 20 years, I recognized a story when I saw it. Hockey players who had been trained by Nancy encouraged me to keep going; they said it was more than just an article. Friends of Nancy and news media that I interviewed said, "It's about time someone told her story."

Research began with the Harris-Burggraf clan, who can best be described as competitive-with-a-capital-C. The family is full of Division I athletes in hockey. Nancy's nephew John Harris, from Minnesota, played golf on the U.S. Walker Team Cup and won the U.S. Amateur Open. Her niece Nancy Harris has won the Minnesota Amateur Golf Championship five times and is married to Paul Blanchard, son of former Yankee great John Blanchard. Nancy's brother Bob played hockey at Minnesota, and Nancy's three sons played hockey at the

University of North Dakota. Daughters Becky and Sally ("Cook") followed in the Harris dental tradition and became dental hygienists. Becky is also a certified NCAA college soccer referee.

Following this preliminary research, I worked with students Hannah Dahl, Sarah McCurdy, Christopher Mohs, and Joshua Clauson to create a one-hour documentary, *Nancy Burggraf: Power & Stride*. They also collaborated on research for the book.

That's how Nancy Harris Burggraf came to live with me. Holding her sweatpants up to me, I know that they would fit. Her ice skates are my size, and I carry my research in her Burggraf Skating Skills bag. Intuitively, she guides this project. She loved her family, hometown, friends, faith, and her hockey players. And she loved to push her own body, which would turn against her all too soon.

Welcome to the story of Nancy Burggraf, a journey not without its struggles, but nevertheless a journey into the light. My speech student was right. Nancy Burggraf should be famous.

Puck Paradise

—◦⌒◦⌒◦—

"Scoreboards are where the mistakes are kept. Expect, accept,
and learn from mistakes, and forget them in two seconds.
You can't carry the guilt." —Burggraf Skating Skills

February 1999

They knocked quietly at first, then louder, respecting the hospital sign, "Family Members Only." Fortunately, the six boys knew they were like family. It wasn't easy for 17- and 18-year-olds to see their guru, a 68-year-old grandma who could out-skate them only a few months earlier, wasting away. A white blanket covered her tiny 5'3", 110-pound frame. Even though she had an IV in her arm, they knew her spirit was not wasting away; it was still sharp and quick. The flowers and plants lining the windowsill and a basket overflowing with cards and letters somehow gave them hope in the dimly lit room.

They came with important news that day. They dropped their jackets on a chair, took off their stocking caps revealing wild, frizzy hockey hair and formed a circle around her bed. The room smelled spicy, like her—not a like a hospital at all. This scent always met them at the rink when they filed in for practice, and they knew she was on the ice even before they saw her.

This was state tournament week, the week it would all come together. She had molded the pieces since they were just seven years old. She taught them about skating their edges, perfecting body techniques, working their power and stride, and perfecting basic techniques.

One after the other, they gently touched her hands and noticed that she still wore her signature rings, one on each finger, the same rings she wore at every practice. They placed a hockey stick across her hands, and her eyes widened as she mustered a small thumbs-up sign. One, two, three, four, five, six times she found strength to tap goals into the stick for good luck and high scoring, a ritual the Roseau Rams had practiced before games during this 1999 season.

"We have something to tell you," said Phil, one of the team captains. "A surprise."

• • •

Outside the hospital window, the February wind whipped across the frying pan landscape of Highway 11 and Roseau, Minnesota, population 2,800. Some old timers joke that up north there are "nine months of winter and three months of bad weather." Although most Roseau-ites enjoy playing a few rounds at the golf course in the summer and spending time outdoors during hunting and fishing season, enthusiasm starts to lag when it comes to sports other than hockey. "Being a basketball fan in Roseau is like being a Baptist in Rome," quipped one resident. "Hockey is more like a religion than a sport," said another. Earl's Drive Inn, home of the Hi Boy Burger, closes every winter with a sign outside that reads, "Closed so we can watch hockey." The concession stand at the Roseau arena boasts being the #1-ranked concession stand in the land of 10,000 rinks.

It's "puck paradise," just ten miles and a slap shot from Canada. Driving along Highway 11, on the very top of Minnesota, a single lonely light is visible between the road and the horizon. When winter wind blows and it feels unbearably

Winter in Roseau in the 1960s.

Cleaning up main street after a winter storm.

cold and lonely, Roseau residents bundle up, go outside, and confront it.

It's a tradition for parents to lace up their kids in double-bladed skates even before they can walk; hockey skates are the next step and snowmobiles soon after that. If you listen carefully, you can hear the winter sounds of Roseau. The swoosh of skates, the whir of the Zamboni, and the mechanic whine of snowmobiles. Signs on the edge of town toast Roseau as the "Snowmobile Capital of the World" (snowmobiles were invented here) and the "Hockey Town of Champions."

The current arena built in 1949 to honor veterans.

Former professional players, who live and work in Roseau, have played with the Chicago Blackhawks, Kansas City Scouts, Minnesota North Stars, New Jersey Devils, New York Rangers, St. Louis Blues, Hartford Whalers, Toronto Maple Leafs, Calgary Flames, Dallas Stars, and Washington Capitals. They have played on the collegiate level for the University of Wisconsin, Minnesota, North Dakota, Colorado, Army, Yale, Colorado, Duluth, Bemidji, Mankato, and the list goes on.

All of them trained with the Roseau Rams, who have won seven state championships, have five runner-up titles, and have played in the state tournament more than any team in Minnesota. Residents joke that they are like Hoosiers on ice. Not content to skate against the small schools in Minnesota, Roseau skates one division up, against Minneapolis, St. Paul, Rochester, and other big city schools.

They developed their lean, quick, strong skating at the indoor Memorial Arena built in 1949 to honor war veterans. If these arena walls could talk, or rather cheer, the energy, excitement, and adrenaline coursing through this building would be palpable. Along the long, concrete hallway are framed pictures and short biographies of the best Roseau players; engraved on the Wall of Fame are names of numerous Olympians, such as 1976 Olympians Rob Harris, Gary Ross, and Blaine Comstock, 1948 and 1954 Olympian Rube Bjorkman, 1964 and 1968 Olympian Don Ross, 1968 Olympian Larry Stordahl, and 1980 Olympic "Dream Team" member Neal Broten.

Down the street from the arena stands the store that was more than a store, what was, until 1998, "Burggraf's of Roseau." The sign outside used to say "Burggraf's—The Clothing People," and it had the community ambiance of a town square or a barbershop. Customers stopped in for new socks and ended up talking about politics and sports, especially hockey, and then buying a suit. Local college kids checked in there when they came home on breaks. Bernie Burggraf, store owner and former mayor of Roseau, and his wife Nancy always had time for kids and also brought a sense of style to Roseau.

Nancy claimed a corner of the store for her fashionable women's wear. Customers remarked that nothing about her—not even a strand of her short cropped hair—was ever out of place, and that included her store. She folded, dusted, and rearranged her merchandize several times each day. It had to be just right.

Nothing about Nancy's inventive power skating techniques was ever out of place either, and her players had to skate just right to develop explosive power and stride. She was rink tough, having trained most of the collegiate and professional players who came to the arena, and she was the first woman to be nominated to the U.S. Hockey Hall of Fame. Through her camps, clinics, and schools, Nancy's touched the lives of a total of 45,000 players over nearly five decades.

She was, in short, a power skating legend.

2

A Secret Weapon?

"I'd like to see the cheap shot go out of hockey. It's the guy who gets beat and becomes frustrated who becomes the goon. He has less skating ability, and to prove himself, he retaliates. The good skater doesn't have to do that. I'd like to see hockey get back to being a game of beautiful skating and passing."
—Nancy Burggraf, during a break in power
skating sessions at the University of North Dakota

February 1999

Phil Larson sat in the chair between her hospital bed and a stand that had a dry-erase board to write messages on and ice chips for Nancy. The butterflies in his stomach jittered about the state tournament the next week, but he was also excited to tell her the surprise.

While he waited for Bernie to come back, memories drifted in and out about early days training with Nancy at the arena. Hockey's lessons, he remembered, had become life's lessons too. One day, as the kids were filing off the ice, a little 9-year-old Squirt player came crying, "Somebody took my best baseball cards. They were my Twins cards."

Nancy whistled the group of skaters all to attention. "Everyone back on the ice."

She scanned the semi-circle around her, looking each of them directly in the eye.

"One of you took something that didn't belong to you." More scanning. The kids' eyes dropped to the ice.

"You need to feel very badly about this. We are a team. Teams don't take from each other. I'm very disappointed in you. Please return what doesn't belong to you. Do the right thing. You can leave now." And that was it. They left in silence.

It was pretty quiet in the locker room. Phil never found out who took the cards, but the boys made a pact that no one in that group would ever betray each other's trust.

1971

The door to training the boys in power skating officially opened for Nancy in 1971 when the new Roseau Rams head coach Terry Abram invited her for coffee. He had a plan. Having played for the University of North Dakota, Terry witnessed how UND players who had trained with Nancy at the arena figure skating school seemed to have an edge on finesse. Terry wanted to go further, and he wondered if this little dynamo on skates could be a secret weapon for the Ram's team. He proposed the plan as she stirred her coffee.

"I'm a woman and I wear figure skates," she smiled, her face tan from a summer of water skiing on Lake of the Woods.

"I need your perfection," he said, "your technique."

"I'll do drills no one else is doing, and they won't be easy," Nancy responded.

"It's worth a try," Terry said. "I'll take the heat. And by the way, I can't pay."

Without hesitating, Nancy shrugged, "I'll do it for the kids."

After that, Terry mandated that all Roseau High School hockey players go through Nancy's pre-season training, called power skating. For the next five years Terry fielded complaints from parents who didn't want their boys trained by "some lady" in figure skates.

"If your boys want to play hockey for Roseau, your sons *will* go through Nancy's program," Terry held fast. "You have to trust us."

On the ice, the whispers were purposefully just loud enough for Nancy to hear. "She doesn't know what she's doing. . . . My dad says this is a waste of time."

She responded to the ridicule in a deliberately soft tone. "Hey, this is what you have to do to be a better player," she explained.

"Right," they whispered, eyes rolling. "Geez, I'm getting chewed out by some lady."

Nancy's power skating mission was to teach kids who already thought they could skate to develop their power and stride for maximum efficiency on the ice. They snickered but the end of practice found them hanging over the boards exhausted while Nancy still skated strong, hardly drawing a breath. Session after session, she skated them into the ice. Power skating taught endurance; she was their role model, and she left no doubt that she loved and cared for the skaters even when she knew she was being laughed at by players, parents, and hockey veterans alike.

Nancy worked the high school pre-season practice, and once the season began, focused on power skating the day before each game. Power skating gave players rhythm, balance, agility, power, quickness, flexibility, and endurance. She taught her players to skate forward, backward, and laterally, to do crossovers both ways, perform two-foot stops both ways, learn to use the inside and outside edges of the blades, run on the toes, do figure eights both forward and backward and other figure skating techniques. She combined basic figure skating patterns with power skating drills, and she always took to the ice in figure skates with a hockey stick in her gloved hands.

The boys who listened to Nancy found they could skate through other players and leave them twisted like pretzels. These players told teammates who doubted, "Shut up and listen." Beyond the obvious efficacy of her program, Nancy's demeanor commanded respect. She didn't carry a whistle; she had her own natural one. And she used it. When she curled both lips together and emitted that shrill blast, the boys skated to attention. They knew she meant business.

Later in the 1970s, when Nancy's power skating techniques had gradually become more accepted, several Roseau hockey fathers approached her to teach power skating to younger kids. So she began classes for 200 players, some as young as preschoolers. Each player paid one dollar to register for the year, and the money was used to buy equipment and the big sign at the end of the arena that proclaimed the rink "Home to Roseau Hockey." Nancy still volunteered all her time, finding her rewards watching the kids who once had to hold onto the boards glide down the ice effortlessly backward and forward.

3

A Student of the Game

"Keep your stick down and your head up." —Burggraf Skating Skills

February 1999

"Hey, boys," Bernie came through the hospital door. "Got your game faces packed? Gotta keep the stick down and the head up, you know. Gotta skate your edges. Explode out there. Show those big city boys a thing or two."

"Are ya comin' down to the game, Bernie?" asked Phil, knowing that Bernie and Nancy had never missed a state hockey game for as long as he could remember. Bernie had even announced the games at the state tourney on occasion, just like he called every home game at the Memorial Arena.

"Can't, guys," Bernie said. "Gotta stay here and watch with Nancy this time. We always watch together. But you know, we're right there with you." The boys nodded in understanding.

"Nancy, here's the surprise," said Phil. "The team is dedicating this tournament to you. And we'll win it for you. We know you'll be watchin'. We'll do it for you."

Nancy pointed weakly to her writing board and Bernie retrieved it. "Jake, keep your head up," she wrote. At 5'-7", goalie Jake Brandt was the shortest kid on the team but an inspirational leader. Nancy liked to work with him and the smaller kids to make them quicker players so they could compete against the bigger players in college and the pros. Jake was a fun kid who loved the game. He hated to lose but kept smiling no matter what.

"I'm gettin' a shut-out for you," Jake said, grinning.

Nancy managed a smiled and raised her thumb.

1900–1940s

Roseau hockey had followed the railroad south from Winnipeg, Canada, to northern Minnesota in 1906 when Archie and Art Alley brought sticks and a puck cut from a tree to local boys playing tag on the Roseau River. The year 1908 marked the first match-up with neighboring archrival Warroad, just east on Highway 11. Roseau won. High school hockey has been played in Roseau since 1916, and by 1920 Roseau had a lighted rink. Typically, when the men finished playing men's league hockey, the local kids climbed over the boards and practiced by moonlight. In 1922, the first indoor hockey arena was constructed, and a grade school hockey program started with help from the American Legion. Early high school players had no uniforms or equipment, so they just wore their school clothes in

The first Roseau Arena, built in 1925 and destroyed by high winds in 1943.

hockey games. Homemade protective gear consisted of willow branches sewn into clothes and the *Saturday Evening Post* strapped in strategic locations.

Nancy Harris Burggraf was born into the Roseau Hockey tradition on May 15, 1930. Bergetta, Nancy's mother, strapped double-bladed skates on her when she was about three years old. Along with older brother Bob and younger sister Sally, the Harris family skated on the Roseau River near their home. Bonfires, fueled by beat-up and discarded skates, flickered along the riverbank on cold winter evenings. Kids used those bonfires to warm up their half-frozen fingers and toes after hours of skating. In her grade school years, girlfriends noticed how Nancy stood out from the other skaters. In her white skates and short skirt, she skated at amazing speeds both backward and forward. With one leg out behind her and her arms flung wide, she did the "Flying Dutchman" maneuver especially well.

Smooth and graceful, she helped the younger children, who were just learning to skate, and taught the more advanced skaters new moves and leaps that she figured out from books. The boys stopped and watched, admiring her skills but never complimenting her. Eventually she became a hockey cheerleader—she did not complain or ask about playing hockey because it was not available for girls. It was thought to involve "too much contact." Instead, young Nancy dreamed of someday auditioning for the biggest national show in figure skating, the Ice Capades.

On Saturday nights, families packed the Memorial Arena rink so tightly that it was hard to get a good stride going, and the temperature soared from all the warm bodies. Twenty-five cents for adults and ten cents for kids bought skaters a night of gliding round and round, mostly to the right. A whistle blew at 8:30 p.m., signaling that children needed to leave the arena. Sometimes a group of skaters in the center of the oval would be up to "monkey business," trying to knock each other over, but mostly it was good family fun.

Nancy's father, the head of the Harris clan, Dr. Richard Van Sant "RV" Harris, graduated from Northwestern University Dental School in Evanston, Illinois, and set up his first practice in his hometown of Morris, Minnesota. He became one of six Harris family members practicing dentistry in Minnesota. In 1922, a traveling salesman came through Morris and told RV about a nice Minnesota town that needed a dentist. With $100 in his pocket, RV moved to Roseau. At that time, the World War I veteran found Highway 11 to be little more than a dirt road, but he was quite taken with the people of Roseau. As a high school student, Bergetta Sorenson applied soon after the practice opened to be RV's dental assistant, and on April 5, 1928, she and RV were married.

Caring for thousands of patients, RV's hardest work was with difficult jaw fractures from accidents—there were no dental specialists at the time. Eventually he invented a special device to help restructure fractured jaws. Ill-fitting, mail-order teeth were also a plague to RV. When he tried to help patients with them, they would blame him for the poor fit. He finally refused to work on them. He once asked a big gruff patient to open his mouth wider, to which the man replied, "You are going to stand on the outside, aren't you?"

RV also invented the "frost shield," a windshield strip that prevented cars from frosting up on a cold winter morning. In 1926, he wrote about getting a patent but threw the papers away. Later he learned that someone else had secured the patent.

RV and Bergetta enjoyed their Rocky Point cabin and boat on Lake of the Woods, and in his twilight years he often said, "I should have taken more time off from work." Having an ongoing vision for a better Roseau, he served on the school board as well as on the State Board of Dental Examiners. He also took local criticism for expansion work and consolidation of schools. He successfully promoted the building of a golf course in Roseau after his sister, who was visiting from Chicago, found her lost golf ball in the middle of a steaming cow pie on the improvised fairgrounds golf course.

Bergetta worked side by side with RV doing lab work and bookkeeping, checking in patients, cleaning the office, and doing just about everything else for twenty-five years. A community activist, she brought the first library to Roseau, and she also served as the first female president of Messiah Lutheran Church. The community remembered Bergetta was a stubborn, and sometimes out of control, hockey fan who made sure the referees knew her opinion on penalty calls. RV often avoided sitting next to her at games. During one game,

Mainstreet, Roseau.

Bergetta turned around and threw a cup of coffee on an opposing fan who had been yelling obscenities at Roseau players.

With long work days at the dental office, responsibilities fell to the children to keep the house in order. Sally, the youngest, called the office countless times to tattle: "Bob is calling me names," or "Nancy is being mean to me." Bob and Nancy christened Sally "Little Piss" because they had to haul her everywhere with them. Nancy and Sally referred to Bob as "King Tut" behind his back. Nancy kept the house spotless, wanting everything to be perfect and up to her parent's strict standards. She often worried that she wasn't quite good enough for her father.

In school, Nancy had difficulty understanding science and math, which frustrated RV because those subjects came easily for Sally and Bob.

"Why are you so dumb about this? " RV asked Nancy one night as they sat at the kitchen table. "Bring the marbles, Mother," RV ordered Bergetta.

"See these seven marbles?" RV set the marbles out on the table. "Two times this many marbles is fourteen," and he brought out

13

seven more marbles. "And times three is twenty-one." Seven more marbles appeared.

Nancy tried her best but often just did not get it. Pleasing her father became a rudder that steered her life toward perfectionism in hockey, her work in the store, and her faith.

Although strict with his children, RV was also remembered for his sense of humor. One Halloween, RV made a set of fake teeth for Nancy. The teeth completely changed the shape of Nancy's face, giving her huge buckteeth and an entirely different appearance. RV took Nancy to a party and passed her off as a relative from another town, and no one in Roseau ever figured out it was Nancy. The fake teeth became famous and were passed around the Harris family when anyone wanted to play a practical joke.

Nancy inherited her father's sense of humor and his knack for problem-solving; from her mother she gained a sense of responsibility. She sat night after night listening to RV and Bob talk over strategies and techniques of Roseau Ram hockey. What would have worked better? What should the coaches have done? She became a student of the game.

"She Was a Scalawag"

"Do it, know it, sense it, try it." —Nancy Burggraf

February 1999

Standing close to her hospital bed, Jake studied her small folded hands and remembered one day when his 11-year-old Bantam boy's team felt pretty cocky at practice with Nancy. They were going through drill after drill effortlessly.

"We're really sick of this," they whined. "We don't want to do this stupid stuff anymore."

Nancy dropped her stick, opened the door, and walked off the ice. She started to untie her laces. The boys stood there looking at each other. One player finally dared to approach Nancy.

"You guys do what I tell you to do because I know what I'm doing," she said to him. "You're too young to realize what you've got and how to use it. That's what I'm here for."

Nancy came back on the ice and said she would continue if all the boys apologized to her personally.

"I'm sorry, Mrs. Burggraf," each boy said solemnly as he skated to Nancy, and again and again and again until all of them had apologized.

Then Nancy picked up like nothing had ever happened and continued the session.

1940s–1950s

In the summer, the Burggraf sisters played house with girlfriends and swam in lakes and rivers. For two weeks, the Harris family took refuge at the Rocky Point cabin about thirty miles northeast of Roseau. When Nancy was a senior, Bergetta allowed her and Sally, a seventh grader, to spend days alone at the cabin where they sunbathed nude on the dock. The sisters bonded at the lake, and Sally looked up to Nancy as her idol. "She knew how to do everything, and she knew how to be in this world," Sally said, adding that Nancy had the ability to learn from a book and was unusually observant.

During the fall of Nancy's eighth grade year, her brother Bob and his friend Gerry purchased a jalopy, a Ford Model-T about mid-1920s vintage. The car had undergone several remodelings, having seemingly been a pick-up and then a rural mail carrier vehicle with unique sliding doors. The seller had explained that the motor's head was cracked, and that he had found a used head, which the boys would need to install before the vehicle would work.

Bob and Gerry towed the car to the backyard of the Harris home, where they started the repairs while Nancy watched.

"I've got the damaged head," said Bob. "Bring the new one."

"It's still not working," said Gerry, frustrated after several attempts at installing it.

They continued to struggle because the bolts would not go in all the way.

"I think we gotta take 'em to be shortened," Bob suggested.

Nancy piped up, "I think the problem is with the head, not the bolts. It's not the same size head."

"Whaddaya know about cars?" Bob rolled his eyes. He and Gerry compared the heads.

"Shoot, they are a different thickness," said Gerry. His face glowed red that a girl had somehow figured this out. They had been trying to replace a low-compression head (a thicker one) with a high-compression one (thinner). Nancy was right, but they didn't want to admit it.

At home, when Nancy took over the housekeeping chores, she became a "cleaning freak," according to her siblings. "If I left my

toothbrush out, she'd throw it away," Bob said, "and if I brought in grass on my shoes, she'd go nuts."

When a high school girlfriend asked Nancy what she would do with a free day, Nancy laughed and said, "Work." She didn't, however, complain about her workload. Although she did become a cover-up expert—if guests (especially the minister) dropped in at the last minute, she would jam everything into the hall closet.

The sisters shared a room in the Harris' three-bedroom white house by the river, and the home became a place where other kids liked to congregate. They fixed up the basement and put in a wood stove, which made it a toasty place for gatherings. Bergetta and RV liked to have their kids at home and other kids visiting.

"Bergetta could be fierce in a nice way," said Bob of his mother. "She was dedicated to her family, but she got her way. Dad was more mild-mannered and meticulous. Mom could handle Dad, which sometimes frustrated him. She was protective and proud of her kids, and both of them gave us drive and motivation."

At school, classmates saw Nancy as an average student, who sat back and didn't force herself on people. She didn't have many close friends during her school years, and when Nancy had her feelings hurt, she would mull it over forever. She was sensitive and often hurt by others. She believed in serving her family and others, and was a peacemaker to a fault, trying to make everyone happy.

Nancy, also known as Nan in high school, attended church activities, sang in the girls' glee club, girls' sextet, and mixed chorus, and played in the band. She acted in the junior class play, participated in GAA (Girls' Athletic Association), was a four-year cheerleader, played basketball, and ran track. She wrote for the yearbook and school paper and was a member of the office and library clubs. Apparently there was some hazing for the GAA initiation; the 1948 yearbook reported that the new girls braved crispy corn flakes, slimy liver, strong Limburger cheese, and other "delectable" items. The GAA organized bowling teams, which reported "no one with any spectacular averages."

She also joined The Library Club, or the "Hush Society," known for its famous last words, "Shhh—not so noisy, please!" Members assisted

The school the Harris and Burggraf families attended.

the librarian with her duties such as cataloguing books but also took time out for elegant suppers at Christmas and Valentine's Day spread out on the long library tables. As the yearbook stated, "These girls did engage in a few extra-curricular activities because all work and no play makes Jill a dull girl." The seniors of 1948 in Roseau left a message in the choir section of the yearbook, hoping that Roseau would always continue to be musically minded, even though their mixed choir had been hampered by short practice hours conflicting with the boys' sports schedules.

The 1948 Rambler yearbook also stated that six cheerleaders (including Nancy) had been chosen that year by the student body. The job of the cheerleaders was to cheer on the football, basketball, and hockey teams in victory and defeat, "new voices mingling in the bleachers in old, time-worn cheers; hoarse shouts of derision floating out from opposite sides." "Games that would never be forgotten," described the yearbook.

Nancy always looked neat and had nice clothes with short hair and no makeup. She never went for the popular and glamorous "Veronica Lake" look (hair over one side of the face, which blocks one eye). Several boys really liked Nancy, especially her short hair, but

apparently she would "never give them the time of day." Beyond high school activities, Nancy became an excellent golfer.

After graduating in 1948, Nancy followed several other Roseau students to St. Olaf College in Northfield, Minnesota, about 45 miles south of Minneapolis and more than 400 miles away from Roseau. She wanted to go because it was far from home. Bergetta did not want her to go for that very reason and would much rather she had attended Concordia College just three hours south of Roseau in Moorhead, Minnesota. But Nancy looked forward the independence and fun that came with distance.

Dar Klemer, Nancy's roommate at St. Olaf, said they hit it off right away, and that Nancy was cute, perky, gregarious, and outgoing with a small athletic body. She enjoyed life and never spoke badly of others. The two roommates lived in the moment, preferring active social lives to being serious students. They dated a lot and were often seen running up the steps to their dorm, hoping they would make the 11 p.m. weekend curfew. Dar called Nancy a "scalawag" and would cover for her when she was late for curfew by putting a pillow in Nancy's bed to make it look like she was asleep. Besides dating, the girls' favorite activity was tanning. They donned their bikinis and lay on the balcony, not just for the sun, but to get the attention of the young men who hooted and hollered at them from below the balcony. College photos showed pictures of the roommates posing on the balcony and showing off their tan lines.

During those years at St. Olaf, as at many colleges, men didn't have many rules, but women were sheltered. Taking advantage of the newly developed GI Bill, older veterans arrived on campus a few years after World War II and they made up 57 percent of the total enrollment at St. Olaf. The sharp increase in male students brought excitement and newness to the campus and to Nancy and Dar. College officials felt that strict rules could not be applied to older men who had been at war serving the country. So, they tried to isolate the female students with stricter visitation and curfew hours. According to the St. Olaf catalog of 1948-1949, none of the students were allowed to have cars, attend dances, or take phone calls after 10 p.m., and smoking by women students was not in harmony with the standards of the college. All students received assigned seats for mandatory chapel; there were special passes for the library and a 7:30 p.m. curfew for women on weeknights. But these rules did not stop Dar and Nancy. The young women were in their rooms for bed check and out as quickly as possible after that. They found entrances for heating tunnels that ran underneath St. Olaf, and that was where they met their boyfriends.

An excerpt from the 1947 St. Olaf handbook told "fellows" the proper protocol for picking up their dates at the dorm.

Go to the dorm in which your date lives. You may meet the housemother, and you'll want to know her. Sit in the parlor and wait. Relax; you'll be there for 15-30 minutes. No smoking. When your date "sweeps" down the staircase and signs out, you are on your own. One tip: you can't call the dorms during study hours from 7:30-10:30 p.m. unless it's an emergency. Grandmothers who die often and on the spur of the moment are not considered an "emergency."

Nancy, who hated waking up early in the morning, always seemed to get stuck with early classes, so she recruited Dar to help her. Dar set their metal wastebasket upside down in the corner by the door and put the alarm clock on top. That clanging sound got Nancy up and going in the morning. Instead of going to the cafeteria for breakfast, the girls ate peanut butter on gingersnap cookies and drank a Coke.

On weekends, the girls took shopping adventures to Minneapolis and bought clothes in the downtown department stores. Nancy had bills for purchases sent to her father in Roseau, where he would subsequently "blow his top" at the amount she had charged to him. In her first semester, Nancy barely scraped by academically at St. Olaf, and at the end of the year she was, in her sister's words, "invited not to return" the following year.

"I admired her free spirit and still kept her on a pedestal," said Sally.

Bergetta was actually pleased because now Nancy would attend Concordia after all and be closer to home. One can only imagine that RV was grateful his department store bills would be lower.

While at St. Olaf, Dar never remembered Nancy skating, or even talking about skating or her dream of being in the Ice Capades. In later years, Nancy's work in the hockey world came as a complete surprise to Dar.

Nancy transferred to Concordia College and attended from 1949-1951, where she declared an English major and continued taking organ and piano lessons. Nancy still didn't mind cutting a few classes now and then to sunbathe and spend time with friends. She was a cheerleader in her junior and senior years, and she was a member of the literary society, Lamda Delta Sigma. She served on the homecoming committee and was also a candidate for Ice Carnival queen in February of 1950.

In a February issue of the 1951 *Concordian* newspaper, an article titled "More Cobbers Receive Diamonds" reported that Nancy Harris became engaged on February 8 and was to be married to her Concordia sweetheart, Clarence "Bernie" Burggraf, son of Pearl M. Burggraf of Stephen, Minnesota. Bernie, a junior business education and psychology major from a small town near Roseau, had aspirations of owning his own clothing store. Active in the Alpha Epsilon Society, Bernie also participated in intramural sports.

Bergetta wrote a note to Bernie shortly thereafter, welcoming him to the Harris family:

Bernie, you are truly welcome to our Nancy. However, I know you understand there is a certain tie to us that I hope will never be lost. Our daughter is very dear to us of course, and we are naturally very concerned with her future. We have always been more or less fussy about her associates, especially her boyfriends and have felt very composed about her association with you. We like you very much, Bernie, and welcome you with open arms as a prospective son. In giving you this green light, we feel rather than losing a daughter we are acquiring a son. I hope that you are both happy and it will be like that for all of your lives together. Today is skating day. Suppose I'd better drag myself down and try to feel young again. Love, Bergetta

Bernie's mother, Pearl, a widow since Bernie's early childhood, composed a note to Nancy following the engagement announcement:

Dear Nancy, I wish everything good for you and Bernie. I do hope Bernie will work and make you proud of him. Roseau plays here on Friday and I hope your folks can come over for coffee. I think I'll have to have Bernie home on Sunday before long to get a bunch of things done that need to be taken care of. Must get to work. Show Bernie this letter; then I won't write another today. We will be thrilled to see you and Bernie when you come home. Love, Pearl

The wedding date had been planned for the summer of Nancy and Bernie's college graduation in 1952. Plans had to be fast forwarded a bit, however, when the couple found out in the fall of 1951 that Nancy was pregnant with their first daughter Rebecca (Becky). Concordia rules dictated at that time that no female student could remain a student while pregnant. Nancy, however, made her own decision to drop out of school to focus on the wedding plans and family. The couple felt it the right and proper thing to do. The couple was married in Roseau on December 29, 1951, and Bernie completed his Concordia studies in the spring of 1952.

Becky was born in June of 1952, and Bergetta wrote a note to the "darling" new little "Mother, Daddy, and Becky":

You would think that a Grandmother would and should have all the time in the world to write letters to her children in their new role in life, but this one is different I guess. How do you feel? No matter how good, take it easy. You are a queen now and enjoy your rest while you can. There will be plenty of time for work later on. Lots of it too; believe me I know. We are very happy for you both, and we will come and see you when we can. In the meantime, give my little darling a big squeeze from this grandmother.

Move to the Star City

"My mom had two speeds, fast and faster." —Frank Burggraf

March 1999

Dressed in their Ram-green blazers, purchased at Burggraf's store, the team left for the Minnesota State AA Hockey Championships at the Target Center in Minneapolis. About the same time, flowers arrived at the Roseau Area Hospital with a card that read, "Nancy, we love you. We will win it for you. Your Rams Hockey Team."

That year, 1999, the Rams were ranked #1 for most of the season. Their only loss came against Greenway Coleraine. The Rams had slim, lean, high-speed skaters. They surprised opponents with their size, strength, and rare ability to skate as well as hit.

"We rely on great speed," said Coach Bruce Olson. "We play simple, strong hockey, wearing the opponent down. We try to play a pass and finesse game but can grind it down when we have to."

The Roseau team was always able to play indoors during official practices at Memorial Arena. But in private hours from 7 to 9 p.m., these kids could practice at an adjacent rink, the north rink called the Dome. At these after-hour pick-up games the team learned to anticipate and read the situation, something Coach Bruce says cannot be taught. "At evening pick-up," he said, "that's where you learn where to go and how to do simple things, like don't move if you're open."

1950s-1960s

Bernie's original vision of owning a clothing store came with him when he, Nancy, and Becky moved to Roseau in 1952. His uncle had owned a clothing store where Bernie had worked as a boy, and he remembered salesmen stopping by the store and talking about Roseau as a "Star City of the North." When the young family arrived in Roseau, two men, Jack Delmore and Herb Borah, lured Bernie into the Roseau business community by asking him to run their grocery store. Bernie managed that store, "Bernie's Fairway Market," and "J&B Sporting Goods" before realizing his dream of owning his own clothing store. Bernie moved "Burggraf's of Roseau" up and down Main Street a few times until 1968 when its location became fixed at the center of Main Street.

Nancy, with household chores and responsibilities of a growing family (five children in eight years) nearly became a recluse in her own home during the 1950s. Becky was followed by: Rick in 1953, Sally (Cook) in 1955, Charlie in 1957, and Frank in 1960.

A busy shopping day in downtown Roseau in the 1950s.

The family lived across the alley from RV and Bergetta and across the street from Nancy's brother Bob, his wife Phyllis, and their five children. After a highly successful four-year stint skating for the University of Minnesota, Bob had passed up Olympic hockey opportunities to go to dental school and returned to Roseau to practice with his father. It had been a tough decision for Bob to turn down Olympic hockey, but his parents convinced him to return to Roseau and help run the business.

Bernie Burggraf with Jim Adelson from KXJB TV for Sports Banquet Night, 1969.

Charlie had vivid memories of living close to his cousins and his first childhood home—the little yellow house behind Bergetta and RV's house. Cash flow for the Burggrafs and the store was tight, so five kids shared one bedroom for a while. Charlie thought Nancy pressured Bernie to find something bigger for the family. The family moved to the old Hansel house on Third Street, and even though it was significantly bigger than the first house, the brothers still had to double up on rooms.

"It was a nice neighborhood," Charlie recalled. "It was the *Leave It To Beaver* days. We lived in one house with five kids: the neighbors next to us had five kids, and the Harrises lived next to them and they had five kids. Lots of games at night."

Charlie suspected that this was similar to the way his mother, Sally, and Bob had grown up, going to the arena and playing the same kinds of games. Things didn't change quickly in Roseau over the decades, and for him it was quite a fun life with abundant family time and the usual activities that revolved around the school and the arena. The Burggraf house had one room in the basement that the kids all remembered, a cistern of some kind a ways below the house that was filled with water, and they couldn't go down there. Of course, the kids conjured all kinds of stories about what was down in that room.

Born at the hospital near the arena during a hockey game on January 18, 1957, Charlie had skates on as soon as he could walk, and his mom bundled up the kids and hauled them to the arena. "Mom loved to skate," Charlie remembers, "and she also wanted to tire out her five kids so she could have some peace at night and we would sleep. Going to the arena was just part of living in Roseau. Gradually we began to play a little hockey."

The Burggraf "bunch" was known to be "aggressive and competitive." It was a family trait to be passionate and to succeed. In the 1960s, as an elementary school player, Charlie had scored eleven goals in one game of Saturday morning hockey. "We won 10-1," Charlie smiled, adding, "I also scored a goal for the other side."

Back in those days, scoring strategy meant a player got the puck and stayed behind his own net, then looked and picked a path to go for the goal. That was Charlie's philosophy: get behind the net and see where everyone was. But in the 10-1 game, Charlie lost sight of the puck and it rolled right between his own goaltender's legs. He said that was the game that started his hockey career.

Nancy and Bernie left the strategy component of hockey alone, preferring to let the coaches deal with that. Before every game, Nancy said to Charlie, "Bust your ass out there"—not usually language his mom would use. "I should have grounded her," he said. "What she meant was, do it hard and do it well regardless of the score. Every shift you go out and you give it everything you have."

The Burggraf household could go from control to chaos in just seconds. Nancy liked order, but it was a constant battle. Her life was a constant balancing act between cleanliness on one end of the scale and Bernie on the other. He was the quintessential salesman, and his desk looked like a bomb had gone off. His desk in the store was "out of bounds" to Nancy's straightening.

On free weekends, the Burggraf family piled into an old station wagon and headed for a drive into Beltrami State Forest. Bernie and Nancy taught their kids gun safety and how to shoot a .22 rifle. Youngest son Frank remembered watching his mom and dad go deer

and goose hunting and being impatient for his chance. At first they let him go with but did not let him carry a gun. "Many times we'd walk out and sit in the sun posting a deer and just fall asleep," Frank remembered of his junior high hunting years. "We were supposed to be hunting, but we'd fall asleep."

One Sunday afternoon, when Nancy shot her first deer, Frank and Bernie, who were a ways from the deer stand, heard two shots and then Nancy's shrill whistle. That meant she had gotten the deer. "When I reached my mom, she was crying," recalled Frank, "and I said to her, 'It's okay, Mom. That means you're not a killer. It's natural. It's a good thing.'" These had been the same words Bernie used to comfort Frank when he cried after shooting his first deer. Oftentimes, Nancy only walked along during the hunt or took photographs in the woods.

Frank also remembered his mother as an avid water skier, who could slalom on one ski and loved trying all kinds of stunts; the family often took the boat out on Lake of the Woods or Maple Lake. Nancy and Frank got the idea that they could ski together and both got on two skis. That well-laid plan resulted in Nancy's legs swiftly splaying out; she hit the water and a groin injury resulted that took a long time to recuperate. Nevertheless, Nancy liked speed, speed, and more speed. Whether on skis, in her car, or on a snowmobile, she liked to push it fast.

"I remember one time," Frank said, "going 85 mph on my snowmobile across a field thinking I was going pretty fast. Suddenly this red snowmobile pulled up alongside of me, and Mom's sitting there and saying, 'Let's go.' So we started going faster and faster racing each other back to our cabin. Dad was pretty upset that we were driving that fast. But we had fun with those snowmobiles. She liked to bend the throttle."

The children saw mellower sides to their parents at bedtime. They could come to their parents' bedside in the evenings and sit on the edge of the bed and talk about whatever happened that day. "If it was about a game," Frank said, "you could spill your guts to them, and they would very calmly put it all in perspective for you. She made me learn to respect my coach's decisions. I remember her willingness to sit and listen."

As Charlie, Rick, and Frank began their Roseau hockey careers, which would eventually lead them all to the UND team and Charlie to the professional ranks in Germany, Nancy became more and more involved in teaching figure skating classes in the community and developing power skating. Daughters Becky and Sally helped their mother with chores at home and also taught at the Roseau Figure Skating Club and organized the annual Ice Revue. Once asked for a newspaper article who the best skaters she ever taught were, Nancy replied, "My daughters, Becky and Sally."

Glitter All Over the Place

"Nancy made the impossible possible for me. When I first went to college, it was the start of the 'burning the bras' era. As far as I'm concerned, Nancy had 'burned the bra' way ahead of that." —Darlyn Marx, teacher and former skater in the Ice Revue

March 1999

Coach Bruce had impressed on his players to put teamwork first. He gave each player a link; when hooked together, they formed a whole chain, a metaphor for teamwork.

"You are individuals," he told the team. "but when you link yourselves together, you become one. You must play together, and there must be no weak link."

The kids hooked their links before each game.

Co-captain Phil said that the idea of a championship had consumed him since he was eight years old. He recalled sitting in section 234 of the old Civic Center in St. Paul watching the Roseau team pick up the championship trophy in 1990. Roseau had also captured the title in the Twin Cities in 1946, '58, '59, and '61. "I'm sick and tired of looking at all the banners in Roseau that we had nothing to do with," he said. "I want to do this for my dad, mom, Roseau, Nancy, everybody." After the 1990 championship, the *Star Tribune* headlines read, "Everything's Comin' Up Roseau." 1999, Phil recalled, was to be Roseau's 28th time in the "Big Show."

Figure skating club, 1956, coached by Nancy Burggraf. "Flowers" for a Cinderella performance, left to right, front: Carol Ness, Center Flower; Carol Miller, Roslyn Dahlquist, Mary Dahlquist, Donna Brandt, Joyce Ness; back row: Rachel Swenson, Shirley Ziska, Bonnie Fertig, Mary Sjoberg, and Arlys Killen.

1950s–1960s

Soon after moving to Roseau, Nancy began developing drills for figure skaters. Her dreams of being in the Ice Capades had ended when she and Bernie started their family, so Nancy created her own version of the dream, the Roseau Figure Skating Club. The club unofficially began with a few girls from a Girl Scout troop, and by 1954 it had grown to 63 skaters. By the late '50s, the club expanded to 255 girls and boys, ages four to adult, who paid $1 a year to belong. Once again, Nancy gave all the money back to the arena.

On Saturday mornings, the arena teemed with over 200 children, scattered around the arena, upstairs and down all at once. As classical music played from the sound booth, some children stretched on the top floor, others went through drills on the ice, while more advanced skaters practiced leaps and turns. All ability levels worked together at one time under Nancy's supervision. Diann Houger grew up skating with Nancy and later became her assistant teacher. She remembered

Nancy as a perfectionist on ice—"she could be in your face and have her arm around you at the same time."

"You did what Nancy said and skated the way she wanted you to," said Diann, who took lessons until she graduated from high school but never had a chance to compete. "I worked really hard under Nancy's mentorship."

Nancy was able to see talent and had a special gift for encouraging it. At the same time, however, she let skaters know if they were doing something wrong. Using her "natural" whistle, Nancy got the skaters' attention, took roll call, and began with a drill. Skaters were quiet out of respect. She knew how to direct practice, and she encouraged all to keep practicing, to slow down and remember to be graceful. Nothing kept Nancy off the ice on Saturday mornings. She kept going even while pregnant with her kids. One day, Nancy fell hard on the ice while pregnant with Frank. She stood up, brushed herself off, and continued directing traffic around the rink.

Eventually it became harder and harder to find ice time for figure skaters as lesson times had been given to hockey programs. It became easy to overlook figure skating, and it was frustrating for the two women.

"I think it was a bunch of dads who never played 'big time hockey' who tried to stop Nancy's influence," said Diann. "Nancy and I had a special closeness."

On Saturdays, Nancy bundled up the five Burggraf children and took them to the arena. It was not uncommon to see the kids taking naps in the penalty box. It became their daycare, and they could play whatever popular music they wanted in the sound room.

Nancy's figure skating club ice show in the 1960s. Joyce Gunderson, Janice Gregerson, Karen Hontvet, Susan Didrikson, Colette Didrikson, Diane Hontvet.

The Ice Revue, the big show, became the most enticing reason for Roseau kids to join the Figure Skating Club. It was a family affair. RV ran the sound system and helped design the set; Bernie was promoter and announcer; Bergetta designed costumes and ran lights, and all five kids skated. Nancy choreographed the numbers with help from Roseau High School theater director Stan Kinderski, and she also designed and sewed costumes. She would order bolts and bolts of glittery fabric from Teener's Costume Shop in Minneapolis, and moms of skaters would bring their sewing machines to the arena on Saturdays to create the costumes.

"The entire practice time and show could be bedlam at times," remembered Diann, whose dad owned the lumberyard and helped build the sets. Nancy traveled to Winnipeg each year to watch the Ice Capades and returned to Roseau with new themes and ideas. "Her choreography was very graceful," said Diann, "and she interpreted the music very well. Her favorite songs were by Neil Diamond— "Cracklin' Rosie" I think—and I just remember there was glitter all over the place."

Diann and her sister skated to "Me and My Shadow" in one of the revues and another time they were dressed as clowns. Nancy always skated a solo number described by viewers as graceful—soft and gentle, like Peggy Fleming. Over the years, as the town enjoyed Nancy's solo performances; she never seemed to age.

Charlie didn't remember the practices much, but he vividly recalled the Ice Revues. "It's funny but I remember the smells," he said, "of make-up and lipstick." Every kid in town was in the revue, and the locker room was full of kids before the show started as Nancy stood on a chair giving out last-minute directions. The arena had locker rooms downstairs, and the kids would have to come up a few steps to their entrance.

"I felt the excitement," said Charlie. "It must be like what professional actors feel when they come on stage. In a unique way it's like playing in the big game. We had practiced; the people were out there and ready for a show, and we performed."

The groups lined up waiting to go out on the ice, and excitement built as they heard the music of the group before them. Then that

group would go off and the next group would come on. It was managed chaos.

Before one show, a little toothless 7-year-old with crossed eyes, thick glasses, and dressed as a teddy bear, looked up at Nancy. She yanked on the fur trim of Nancy's costume.

"Mith Burggraf, Mith Burggraf," she lisped and tugged.

"Just a minute, sweetie," said Nancy, reaching down to tighten the laces on her own skates.

"Mith Burggraf, *Mith Burggraf,*" pleaded the little voice out from under her teddy bear costume; the bear hood had now fallen over one eye. "Ith it time for the teddy bearth yet? Don't forget to tell me."

"Sweetie, see your chair by the other bears? You go sit by them. See Becky? There's Becky," Nancy pointed to her oldest daughter. "She will tell you when to go. Mrs. Burggraf has to skate her solo now."

"Hey, Frank hit me," whined one tin soldier, as he sat in a line of ten other toy soldiers, swinging their skates back and forth underneath green folding chairs. "Mrs. Burggraf, make him stop."

"I have to skate now, Frank. Listen to your sister. Becky, help settle this."

Charlie wondered how his mom found time to do all this, to create and direct two hours of solid program, act after act.

"I was one of the seven dwarfs," he said. "I think I had to sneeze a lot. I must have been Sneezy. Another time I was the back end of a moose or a cow. It was painful because my brother Rick was the front end and we were supposed to sit on something. But he sat on me. I remember this tremendous pain in my back, and I cried underneath there. Just skating around crying."

Frank's first pair of skates were hand-me-downs that provided little ankle support and were finally chewed up by the family's black Lab, Zip. "The arena was our daycare center," he said. "I think some of my pictures show that I was upset to be in the Ice Revue. I was one of the last of the Seven Dwarfs; I think it was Grumpy. My brother said I played the part well."

Frank said he didn't remember what to do when he took to the ice as Grumpy the dwarfs. He fell in the dark and started crying. "This one spotlight followed everybody around the ice," he said. "Suddenly,

I was out of the light. Somebody came out and rescued me, and all of a sudden I ended up back in line."

Rick entered the rink wearing a sombrero and skated to the "Mexican Hat Dance." He also remembered being a cowboy and the front end of a horse that crushed his brother at the back end of the horse. "I remember all the costume sewing Mom did," Rick said. "I thought that's what she did for a living."

It became more than a full-time job for Nancy as she carefully pieced together ideas, sets, costumes, and choreography for each year's theme. For the Ice Revue on March 6, 1956, the theme "Cinderella" featured a prince, princess, mice, pages, coachmen, stepsisters, and a stepmother. Another year, "Holiday on Ice" had changing seasons and performers dressed like snowmen, flowers, valentines, Easter bunnies, and ghosts. "Garden Fantasy" in March of 1957 featured costumed skaters as birds, squirrels, rabbits, ducks, bugs, frogs, elves, sunbeams, flowers, butterflies, and queen bees. In 1959, "Child's Dream" portrayed a sleeping child visited by the sandman as toys, fairies, Raggedy Ann, sugarplums, marching dolls, candy canes, China dolls, snowflakes, and a snow queen paraded through her dreams.

A special effect, the first disco ball in Roseau, wowed the audience as it spun round and round in a rainbow of colors. Pails of dry ice sat near the entrance to give the illusion of skaters emerging from the fog. A very special number ended each program, a precision skating line of twenty girls in formation, dressed in red, white, and blue who skated to Sousa's "Stars and Stripes Forever." Becky was part of the team that skated in circles Rockette-style or in a crack-the-whip line— not an easy task when she was at the end and went flying off. They had to skate furiously to get back in formation. Nancy usually skated her solo and also a duet with Robert Lillo, a local figure skater turned hockey player, to one of her favorite songs, such as "People" or "Somewhere Over the Rainbow."

Over 2,000 people attended the Revues, paying 75 cents for adults and 25 cents for students. Nearly two hours in length, the revue had a 15-minute intermission to recondition the ice. Two skaters carrying flashlights and dressed as fireflies came on the ice in the blackness

and skated before the intermission. In the mid-1950s, a Minneapolis newspaper called the Revue one of the "best amateur ice shows in Minnesota." By the 11th Annual Revue, "Rhapsody on Ice," the show featured colorful lighting and a trip through space in a big rocket, complete with Batman and Robin, a skating trip over the rainbow, Snow White and the Seven Dwarfs, Waltzing Cats, Norwegian dolls, Swiss puppets, and skating Parisians.

Each year the lighting and scenery got more sophisticated. By 1967, the 12th Annual Revue, the scenery changed for each number; the disco ball had been replaced by a giant chandelier that descended from the ceiling; and colored spotlights and strings of white lights circled the arena boards. The finale featured 240 skaters making a serpentine formation on the ice. The newspaper reported "a heavily applauded finale." The Revues were always hampered, however, if Roseau had an unusually warm spring. With no artificial ice, the arena was handicapped for many years by water on the natural ice; puddles had to be swept, pumped, and drained before the production could begin.

During the mid-1960s, Nancy took the show on the road to neighboring Red Lake Falls, Minnesota. She received the following letter from her uncle, a Red Lake Falls dentist:

Dear Nan,
You and your show are the talk of the town. It was so beautifully done. People just can't get over your dedication, both you and Bernie. And then to come out and skate that graceful solo. We are all indebted to you, Nan. We think it's a crime you do this for so little compensation.

Another Red Lake Falls resident wrote to the local newspaper:

Our community is more than buzzing about the professional quality of the show. A person like Nancy is such a tremendous force for good for our young people in these uneasy times. Nancy is really a whole person. Her solo skating was shockingly beautiful and far and away the best number of all.

The Revues were a truly homegrown community project. Nancy also assisted her skaters in passing their preliminary and first tests in figure skating. She brought in judges from Winnipeg for her students, hoping that some might go on to audition for professional ice shows, a dream that could no longer be a reality for her.

Darlyn Marx, an acting and music teacher in Illinois, moved to Roseau as a first grader. "We thought we were stars in that Ice Revue," she said. "No matter how 'plain Jane' we were, Nancy transported us to another world." Darlyn entered the performing arts and received her master's degree in theater because of Nancy's ice shows. She remembered that every kid in Roseau skated and that Nancy had an amazingly calm demeanor, yet got things done. She made each child feel valued.

"We thought we were ballerinas in all that fabric and sequins," Darlyn said. "I got to wear a cute sailor costume in 'Stars and Stripes Forever.' We wore fancy bangles on our wrists and ribbons in our hair. I kept my costumes for years—even the Little Brown Jug outfit. I was really nervous for my solos, and while I was skating, 50 to 60 kids were waiting behind a curtain to go on the ice. It was a huge staging phenomenon."

Nancy helped the young girls in Roseau push the boundaries. They didn't feel common or as though they were from a small speck of a town. She also knew how to help her skaters though all stages of life. "She played on our strengths," remembered Darlyn. "When she taught us, we were auditioning every time we skated, but I never remember being fearful of not making a part. We didn't have to be super talented."

Other skating students reported that Nancy was always there to pick them up if they fell, and she pushed them to the next level. She helped them bond as a group while demanding a lot of them. Darlyn feels she is demanding in her classroom because of Nancy's influence. Other former students said that Nancy was always beautiful in her simplicity. At practices, she wore sweats, blue jeans, and sweatshirts, and she looked gorgeous and put together. Darlyn said Nancy was way ahead of her time, and women Nancy's age were jealous of her; she was talked about endlessly. She was businesslike and confident, and

she got along with men in the business world quite well because she was such a hard worker.

Because of a need for male skating partners in the "Skaters'Waltz" for the Ice Revue, Nancy began to sweet-talk young hockey players into coming to her figure skating classes. It wasn't easy because the players were mostly mad at her for taking up too much of their ice time for the figure skating club.

"We'll do it only if we can wear hockey skates," they had bargained.

"Done," she had agreed.

She taught the hockey players figure skating techniques, to use the inside and outside edges of their blades and how to do a couple of leaps required by the "Skaters' Waltz." Mike Baumgartner, who eventually went on to play in the NHL, discovered it was "kinda fun" to learn to waltz. "I was about in eighth grade when Nancy was trying to convince us to waltz on ice. We thought it was kinda goofy to start with, but there were quite a few of the guys in the show. And she really filled that arena with people. Nancy always had everything in order. She had her life in order."

In the 1960s, these young men who trained in Nancy's club eventually caught the eye of the Roseau and UND hockey coaches. Why were these boys better skaters, with more finesse, more power and balance in their strides? They didn't have to look far to see the common denominator—Nancy Burggraf's training techniques. The skating club and ice revues slowly began to evolve into Burggraf Skating Skills, or what some would eventually call "voodoo hockey."

7

The Store that was More than a Store

"Life is kinda work, work, work." —*Nancy Burggraf*

March 1999

She glanced down at her hands, and then up at the flowers the boys had sent, then at Bernie who was taking a snooze in the lounge chair. She thought of them riding on the bus, looking sharp in their green blazers and fighting hard mentally to calm their nerves. She was nervous too and had several restless nights thinking about the tournament and hoping they would remember their basics. It made her legs twitch all night long.

She remembered starting the little guys skating without sticks so they wouldn't become a crutch for them, so they learned to put power in their stride. She broke techniques down for each individual boy and tried to move from the skills into their minds. She hoped they would remember the "grit" they needed to have in a big game.

When they were tired, she always worked them harder. They had to be able to bend the knee and drive the net. They had to be able to finish. She wished she could whistle and shout like she had a million times, "Move your feet, move, move."

1960s–1970s

When her children were young, Nancy spent most of her weekends at the arena and most of her weekdays at the store. It was the ultimate family business on Main Street and the ultimate in customer service. The family nearly bled to death during the Christmas holidays because they had so many paper cuts from the free gift-wrapping service. The minute Nancy and Bernie thought the kids were old enough, they recruited them for the wrapping brigade.

"Charlie, if you want to be a wrapper, pick up your speed a little bit," said Nancy, watching Charlie fumbling with the tape. "Customers are waiting. You're too messy. Maybe your hands are too big."

Nancy, a perfectionist about free gift wrapping for customers during the holidays, knew what she had to do. Charlie Burggraf admitted defeat that day. He wasn't neat enough and he wasn't fast enough. Was he disappointed? No, not really. He knew there would be plenty of other work for him at the store. Just because he didn't wrap perfectly enough for his mother's standards didn't let him off the hook.

"I didn't make the cut," said Charlie, with a smile. "My mom exiled me from the Christmas wrapping brigade, so I got to make bows instead with the bow machine, hundreds of them every day for the holidays, red, green, and gold. I still remember it was thirteen whacks with that machine to make a bow. Some things stay with you forever." Other kid jobs included waiting on customers, providing free package delivery, cleaning the store, or cooking and cleaning at home.

Frank's main job at the store became clean-up since he was the youngest. He worked the noon-hour shift while his dad and Rick went for lunch. He also helped out during the holidays, which was like "harvest season" for the store, working his way up to wrapping supervisor. He called himself the go-fer who made sure the bow ties were made and that the wrapping paper was stocked.

"Lots of people called Dad and Rick," Frank remembers, "because they knew what people wore, their sizes, and what colors they should wear in the winter and autumn and so forth. I got into it a little bit, but I was never as talented in that as they were."

The Burggraf kids also recalled the hype of Roseau shopping in the days before Christmas. The store closed at about 4 p.m. on Christmas Eve, and the family joined aunts, uncles, and cousins at Grandma Bergetta's house for dinner with Bernie still in his shirt and

Tree Planting. Left to right, back row: John Reese, mayor and depot agent; Minda Bertilrud; Don Funk, manager of Penneys; forestry agent. Front row: forestry agent and Nancy Harris Burggraf.

tie from work. Burggraf family time, time to spend with mom and dad, took place between Christmas and New Year's.

The month of January meant inventory and the annual Burggraf Store Auditorium Sale. The Burggrafs were generally great buyers but sometimes ended up with clothes that didn't sell. The solution to the overstock became the sale at the old city hall, a big white building built in the 1920s. The Burggraf kids hauled merchandise from the store basement, loaded it up, and brought it to the auditorium.

"It was a lot of work," recalled Charlie. "We could just as well have been hauling it from New York to Los Angeles. Loading, unloading, driving the distance."

Townspeople looked forward to the sale all year, but Charlie compared the rigor of the work to having to get up at three in the morning and milk cows. "You bring up all that stuff, all those shoes and then had to move it back again every year if it didn't sell."

At one sale in the 1970s, there were some pretty wild women's shoe styles with gladiator bootstraps and high spike heels. Year after year, the shoes never sold. Finally, tired of hauling the shoes back and forth, Bernie decided they needed to get rid of them. They gave them to the fall church clothing drive. The shoes were headed to a mission in Africa. The following year, during a Sunday church service, Nancy nudged Charlie to make note of an announcement in the bulletin. Messiah Lutheran Church was taking clothing donations for Africa and to please bring donations to the church. In bold letters the announcement said, "No shoes, please!"

"I leaned over to my mom, who was trying not to laugh but had tears streaming down her cheeks," said Charlie, as they envisioned huge refrigerator boxes of strappy spike heels going to Africa a year earlier. "I whispered to Mom to imagine the Africans on a cold night saying, 'Put another shoe on the fire.' I could never imagine the spikes and straps being of much good to them in Africa."

In the store, Nancy took her job seriously. When she was done cleaning, she reorganized the shelves. She kept everything neat "to a fault" and friends, family, and employees said she stressed out too much about the store.

Meanwhile, Frank and Rick invented "store games" when Bernie left them alone to "mind the store."

"Hey, no one's here," Frank would say, feigning surprise. "Time for some baseball."

"Get out the tape wad," said Rick, smiling.

"You're pitchin'," said Frank.

"Get the bat," Rick replied.

Bam! A line drive headed for the front door.

A customer opening the door, extended his hand and caught the ball like nothing.

"Good thing you played baseball," Rick said.

"What time do you boys start the game?" the customer asked.

"Everyday when Dad leaves for coffee," they said.

"I'll wait for him to leave and then I'll be over," he said.

December 1994.
First step: Rick Burggraf.
Second step: Kari Rygh Byfuglien,
Eric Hallie, Katie Burggraf
Stromland. Third step: Joan
Burggraf, Bernie, and Nancy.

One year, Charlie hurt his knee in hockey, and the boys played store hockey with his crutches. Bernie never knew about it.

And there was the banter. A sign on the door read, "Just come in and say hello." And people did. "Bernie's" gave folks a chance to catch up on what was happening in town, catch mumblings on city business, discuss worldviews and sports. People came by the store for Nancy and Bernie. Sure, they needed new clothes; some even said they would go naked if "Bernie's" wasn't in business. The store was one of the first places out-of-town visitors stopped. It made the visit to Roseau official. Visitors knew that Bernie was in the business as much for the chitchat as for the sale. Bernie and Nancy were the town's patriarch and matriarch for kids who came home on college breaks. Kids checked in with them before they made their rounds around town. If Bernie found out that kids were doing something great with their lives, he'd call up the *Roseau Times Region* and send them over for an interview. If customers needed to know anything—where to get a new car, where to take a sweetheart to dinner—"Bernie's" was the place to find out. The store was the place to go for a new suit, a few laughs, some good old-fashioned ear bending, and wisdom.

A sign on the door read, "Shoplifters will be beaten to death."

"You get the same effect with a little humor," Bernie said. They also hung a quote from Williams Jennings Bryan: "Burn down your cities and leave our farms, and your cities will spring up again as if by magic; but destroy our farms, and the grass will grow in the streets of every

city in the country." Burggrafs believed that farmers were the backbone of the store's economy.

The store ended up with a team of four to five high school workers who worked during the summer months. Bernie engrained in the young work force that Burggraf's provided quality at a price they wanted to pay. "As John Ruskin once said," Bernie told his staff, "'I'm too poor to be able to afford cheap clothes.'" The storekeeper also reminded his workers of the biblical customer service imperative for the store: "they came as strangers and we took them in."

A Burggraf employee throughout his high school years, Jeremy Erickson said Bernie could flatter the socks off customers and then sell them new ones. "Bernie entertained the customers while we assisted and rang up sales," recalled Jeremy.

Bernie trained Jeremy in the fine art of salesmanship. "Tell the customer, 'This was made with you in mind; you deserve it.'"

"Make sure they leave with a smile," he told Jeremy. "Don't just sell to sell. Make sure you know who it's for." Bernie was concerned with the way clothes fit a person. There was nothing worse, he believed, than having clothes that didn't fit. The Burggrafs kept their business thriving for 46 years with the motto: "The customer is always first."

"They don't have to come in your store," Bernie said. "You have to make them feel like wanting to come in and have them leave with a smile on their face. You have to serve people. Whatever it takes. And you can't forget that."

In 1976, Nancy, a very good knitter like her mother Bergetta, opened a yarn corner in the store that evolved into a full line of women's high-quality clothing. Her boutique, "Nancy's Country Cove," marketed upscale and expensive brands such as Pendleton, Act III, and Geiger. The store was advertised as the "Biggest little clothing store north of the Cities." Bernie and Nancy knew what would sell; they were tasteful buyers and trendsetters.

"They made everyone in Roseau look good," said one customer. "Nancy and Bernie were like the John and Jackie Kennedy of Roseau, a Camelot couple."

The couple also kept track of local students' successes in academics and athletics and often called coaches around the region

Dale Harkhart from the Minnesota Vikings speaks at an athletic banquet.
Bernie and Nancy are seated to the right.

to suggest they recruit Roseau athletes. Bernie once counted that he and Nancy had helped 42 hockey players from the area get an education at UND. "Nancy and I believed you could do a lot of good if you didn't care who got the credit for it," said Bernie. "Roseau is a small town, and we want our athletes to be recognized. That's why we stayed active with the kids."

The store also sponsored full-page ads in the *Roseau Times Region* featuring new fashion trends with Rick and Becky modeling. In one 1970s ad, Becky was wearing a "4-Alarm Fashion!" The paper described "a mod A-line skirt in Pendelton's plaid—a long, zingy 100-percent wool, snag-proof sweater with Lady Dingo boots, a smashing suede belt and a Dofan leather handbag." In the same ad, Rick sat on the hood of a new Ford Pinto and the copy read,

When the new Ford Pinto and Burggraf's fashions get together, it's the right look for the man on the move. A really high-octane line up of new shirts, sport coats, and slax that will make your fall a real gasser!! Authentic flag colorings give Ricky's boldly striped crewneck sweater, with matching scarf and barret, a colorful international look that's right anywhere. And the Dingo—the now dimension of boots—sets the style pace for the bootman, fast action fashion authority at Burggraf's.

Also in the wedding attire business, Bernie treated every wedding as if it was the only one in the world. Renting tuxedos for out-of-town guests had to be done creatively. The rental call came in to Bernie:

"How does his size compare to Nick or Ole or Pete . . . ?" Bernie would ask.

"Well, he's in between Nick and Pete," the caller might answer. Bernie then adjusted the sizes and saved the sheet.

One time the mother-in-law-to-be told Bernie, "Well, I know the exact size he is."

"I don't think that can be his size," Bernie said, who had met the groom.

"Don't tell *me*," she replied. "I am a seamstress."

So Bernie, good friends with Desmonds, the formal company where they rented the tuxes, ordered two tuxes.

"I want one," he said, "in the size the mother-in-law measured and the one I think is right."

When he presented the one the mother-in-law had ordered, the pants were above the ankles and the groom couldn't button the jacket.

"What happened?" the woman asked.

"It's an art," said Bernie, who knew the woman quite well. "If you know the waist, I can build the guy in between. I ordered another one I thought he should have."

"Everyone left happy," Bernie remembered. "I didn't put her down, and it makes kind of a cute story. We had fun like that in the store; we

Bernie Burggraf and Norman Larson in Buggraf's Store, circa 1970.

had to have fun. You have to remember that if you've got problems, the customers don't want to hear them because they've got problems of their own."

Burggraf's customers also remembered Bernie playing guessing games. When a new customer inquired about a suit, Bernie said, "You must be about a 31-30 and 15 ½, 32 and probably take a 39 short." The customer replied, "How did you know that?"

As sales were being made on the main floor of the store, Nancy's office in the basement functioned as a sanctuary. During his junior and senior years of high school, Jeremy took a break from selling upstairs and visited Nancy in her basement office. "She shared Bible readings with me and encouraged me. Nancy became my spiritual mentor. Our prayer sessions went on for years. When I returned home for the holidays from college, it was routine for me to go down to the basement and find Nancy and pray with her."

The basement was such a quiet spot—a haven for Jeremy. He felt like he was entering the "king's chambers" for counsel. When he left the basement, he always felt like he was a better man as Nancy sent him off with a big hug. His visits with Nancy dramatically influenced his life.

"She always seemed young," he recalled as he described Nancy, "and there was something oddly different about her, even though she was as real as the meat and potatoes we'd have back home on the farm at the end of a long day."

In Jeremy's eyes, Nancy had a deep understanding of God and scriptures, something mystical Jeremy felt had been lost in the faith, which to him had become too routine. Nancy took her cues about having a store with a "mission" from Herdis Reese, a widow and owner of the variety store across the street from Bernie's. Herdis, called the "dime store missionary," was well known for praying with and for her customers. A former Roseau pastor credited Mrs. Reese for his own spiritual awakening and call to attend seminary. Nancy carried on this Main Street legacy.

Along with the theological discussions with Nancy, Jeremy remembered the store as a big, long party from Thanksgiving to Christmas.

"I would ring up a purchase," he said, "throw the purchase in a box, run it upstairs to Nancy to wrap, where she could honestly wrap

about eight presents per minute, then run it back down to the customer. I enjoyed overhearing the conversations she was having with her daughters and grandchildren. It was quite a party."

One Christmas, Nancy presented Jeremy with a devotion book that he uses to this day, *My Utmost for His Highest*. "She was so excited to give it to me," said Jeremy, "because she knew that would fit right in my back pocket."

During another Christmas rush, Jeremy brought another gift for Nancy to wrap. It was the end of the day and Jeremy was very tired. He set the gift on the table and turned to leave. Nancy looked up from her scotch tape and wrap.

"Have you ever wondered what God smells like?" she asked.

Jeremy stopped and looked up at her wondering if she was joking. She was serious, but still had a twinkle in her brown eyes.

"I'm not so sure I've ever wondered that," Jeremy said.

Nancy related two instances when she had caught the fragrance of God. She said at a very special time of worship or prayer she would sense the smell of a robe, like a king had just passed by. It had wafted in her direction. It made sense to Jeremy, as he had watched Nancy hang up incense sachets around the store and eucalyptus branches near the clothes to make them sweet smelling and to promote good health for the customers.

At one point, when Jeremy had a headache, Nancy said to him, "Come here."

He gave her his left hand and described the kind of headache he was having. She took his hand, pinched it near the thumb and said, "Take a deep breath; close your eyes."

After thirty seconds she stopped, looked up, and said, "It's gone, isn't it?"

"Yeah, it's gone. That's better than Tylenol."

"There's sort of this haunting way about Nancy," said Jeremy. "So much that went on inside her head and inside her heart that you never knew. She had this great freedom, great spirit, but she carried this great burden too, and that burden made her soft and incredibly compassionate."

8

The Arena – It's "Nancy Time"

*"She motivated us. We worked so hard. She got the best out of you.
When Nancy was on the ice, you didn't waste time."*
—Paul Baumgartner, member of 1999 Ram's team

March 1999

Jake Brandt took his seat on the bus, ready to roll down Highway 11 toward Minneapolis. Flashbacks of learning hockey as a preschooler made him smile. He always wanted to be a goalie, but his dad didn't let him at first. He thought of Nancy working with him on drills like T-glides and shuffling. *What balance*, he thought. She could skate circles around most of the guys. She could go down on one skate, stick the other skate out in front and "shoot the duck" like it was no problem at all. The rest of them were on their butts. And her unreal but somehow comforting perfume. That's what he remembered most: her smell.

He knew some people didn't believe in Nancy or her techniques, but his team used it as fuel to prove to everyone that she knew what she was doing.

He thought of Roseau and the fans that would be coming to fill the Target Center. It was all about hockey, hockey, hockey. He loved growing up in a place as special as Roseau, and one day when he finally leaves, he knows he will miss it.

1970s–1980s

Whether in the store or on the ice, Nancy became a teacher and mentor for both young and old in Roseau. "It's good to repay Roseau," she said, "for everything it has given me." At the high school, Nancy volunteered as choreographer for *Oklahoma, Music Man, Fiddler on the Roof, Brigadoon,* and *Bye Bye Birdie.* She believed that musicals gave the participants poise and developed voice and acting skills. Plus, productions taught people how to work together. She also advised the cheerleaders and dance team and led a 6 a.m. women's exercise class. From books and tapes she taught herself aerobics, yoga, acupressure, massage, and disco dance.

Back on ice, by the late 1970s, Nancy's Power Skating techniques along with coaching from Terry Abram and Dick Johnson had become engrained in the Roseau Rams training programs for all ages: Mites (6- to 8-year-olds), Squirts (9- to 10-year-olds), Pee Wees (11- to 12-year-olds), Bantam (13- to 14-year-olds), and the high school teams.

"Nancy was a pain for a while at first. It was hard," said Phil Larson. "We couldn't use pucks; we were simply skating. We didn't like that. And then her corny drills ... inside edges, outside edges. But we finally accepted it when it was Nancy time. If we didn't work, she skated us. She slowly came in and gained our respect, and she respected us too."

If Nancy thought players weren't paying attention or screwing around, she said, "All right. I'll teach you young guys what it means to skate." They skated laps or had races or just did stops and starts. She blew her whistle so many times that soon they just wanted to go home.

Nancy always looked unruffled. And the whole rink smelled of her perfume. It wasn't so strong like "oof, lay off," according to the boys; "it was just a soft, 'there's Nancy's smell. It was Nancy time."

Nancy put away sticks and pucks to teach. She also showed her players how to lace skates properly, so the boot of the skate could keep control. And when she let out a shrill whistle, players skated to attention, sometimes 40 of them, from toddlers to high school age. They knew it was time to get down to business. She also used her whistle to change drills. Parents loved it that she had this much

1970s downtown Roseau.

control over the kids. For the players, it was fun to watch Nancy skate. She seemed to float out there, and she could do everything she wanted the boys to do. And the boys told each other if a woman could do something, then they could do it. Nancy had them walking on their toes for strength and coordination. "It was really tough," players concluded. "It's easy to run on your toes, but walking took a while to get used to."

In another drill, Nancy had the boys skate backward, then kick up one leg and keep going down the ice. It took time and patience to learn. She helped the players work on leg extensions and even duct-taped their arms to their sides so they would learn to move with their hips. Sometimes the players were tied to parachutes that served as drag for drills. Nancy's power skating used all kinds of maneuvers, even jumping over and diving under sticks, a new version of a limbo dance on ice. She spent time with techniques that other coaches never thought of doing. At the end of a weeklong training with the boys, Nancy invented an obstacle course to test the skills they had learned. Whoever won the timed race got a hat, T-shirt, stick, aluminum shaft, vitamin C tablets, or some other trinket from Nancy. She kept things competitive.

Nancy did extensive research on what would develop balance and skills in the players. She had a gift; she could read a book, be able to do whatever the book taught, and then apply it practically. She even learned human physiology by reading books.

Andy Lundbom, a Roseau Rams product, graduate of West Point, and later a professional hockey player, first met Nancy at her skating skills clinics in the arena. He noticed that she had a smile on her face every day. Some days she said it was going to be an "easy" workout day—clearly a joke since those days were the toughest. She made even the most strenuous days fun. What amazed Andy was Nancy's small stature compared to her strong skating stride. And for Andy, an efficient stride in a game where every inch counts helped him make it in the pros.

At West Point other players were impressed with Andy's skating and they asked him where he learned to skate. "Nancy taught me," he said.

"You got taught by a woman?"

"You should meet her. It's not the same once you meet her," he replied.

Mike Baumgartner, University of North Dakota hockey player and professional NHL player with Chicago, Dallas, and Kansas City, was born in 1949. Coached by Oscar Almquist, Mike and his teammates began practices in the fall down on the river. They skated on the side of the dam because it would always freeze there before the natural ice in the arena. To the north of the arena was an outdoor rink where Mike lost his first teeth.

"I went through all the Roseau levels of hockey and practiced on the river, rinks, and ponds like all other kids in those days," he said. "Nancy was a really good lady. On the ice, she was a pioneer in power skating, teaching agility, and using the edges to be quicker and stronger. If you can't skate, you can't play the game. As we all got older, we learned to respect her for what she was doing—for being a pioneer."

Mike's son, Paul, a member of the 1999 Roseau Rams High School hockey team, grew up talking hockey at the Burggraf store with Nancy and Bernie. "I remember Nancy being on the ice ever since I remember playing hockey," Paul said. "We used to get so mad at her for taking away our ice time with the figure skating program."

"Right away on the ice you skate round and round to warm up, and then Nancy gave that whistle and we went into drills. Nancy was famous for the four-line drill on one end," said Paul, "where you skate the length of the ice doing a different drill and then back. When we were little we didn't take it very seriously. I whined once or twice, and thought it was kind of a joke. We'd try to make the drills funny, but as we got older we learned how valuable they were. And by high school we were taking them more and more seriously."

The boys voted "shoot the duck"—skating and crouching on one leg while sticking the other leg out in front—as the worst drill. Most kids could eventually do this going forward, but then Nancy encouraged them to do it backwards. As Paul said, "We all went on our butts with that one."

Aaron Broten grew up in Roseau and played hockey for the University of Minnesota. He and his brother Neal turned professional after playing in the 1980 Olympics, and then Aaron went on to play eleven years in the NHL, mostly in New Jersey. Aaron had known the Burggrafs his entire life and felt fortunate to experience Nancy's power skating training in the 1970s as a ninth grader.

"In those days," Aaron reflected, "we were 'old school' players. Hockey wasn't our life. We got a lot of playing time in when there was ice, but when the ice [melted] off the rink, we'd spend ten hours a day on the golf course, or played baseball and fished. It sure has changed now that you can play hockey all year."

Aaron pointed out that hockey is such a fast sport that if players are not good skaters, they will not be able to play. Nancy's drills honed footwork, turning, balance, and edgework. At the professional level that Aaron played, he found that these skills separated good players from the great players. If players could do the finer things, they could excel. Power skating has to do with balance and using edges because not everyone is the same size. A 220-pound player is going to be able to push around a 170-pound player. But if the 170-pound player has a good center of gravity and balance, he can let himself be pushed from any direction. If the player is quicker, he will survive.

Former Olympian Henry Boucha, a Warroad native, also played on the U.S. national team and for the Detroit Red Wings. He graduated in

1969 and did not have the opportunity to work with Nancy but observed her standing at ice level and analyzing young players' skating techniques. Henry explained that a Russian coach actually developed off-ice training in the 1970s when the Russians were dominant on ice.

"The Russian coach combined figure skating with off-ice training and then skated his players for six hours a day," Henry said about early hockey training. "The U.S. and Canadian skaters practiced two hours a day. Who do you think was going to win? The U.S. and Canada realized they needed to make some changes and look at all aspects of the game, including stick handling, skating, off-ice training, nutrition, and classroom. Nancy was a pioneer in these techniques and power skating."

When Nancy saw that a player was struggling with certain techniques, she pulled him aside for a one-on-one talk. She had the ability to analyze any player's style and give them information on how to be better. Nancy believed that hockey was more mental than physical. "You have to think about what you do before you do it," Nancy coached, "and that will make you a better player. It will make you a split second faster than the other guy goin' for the puck."

Every day was positive for Nancy, reflected a former player. Just because the sun didn't shine, if you lost a game, it never meant that you were a loser. She inspired her players to take something positive out of each day. Not every player, of course, that Nancy coached went on to play in college or turn professional—but they were all touched by her drive and enthusiasm. Mike Carlson, a Roseau player, became a sports medicine trainer in the National Hockey League, and he also uses Nancy Burggraf's training techniques with his players.

Mike was about 5 years old when he began skating with Nancy. "I never realized the magnitude of what Nancy was doing until later when I learned she had been training college and professional players," he said. "We didn't know what we had in our backyard all those years."

Nancy could pick apart a stride biomechanically, and she knew how any skater could get the most out of the game and out of his body. It was amazing for Mike to watch.

"One quick whistle," Mike remembered, "and you knew when to skate. That was about it. People got goin'. You didn't mess around with Nancy too much. You toed the line and did what she said."

Nancy demonstrated mental toughness, and she looked right at a player and saw through all the junk that was going on. If a player was cocky or arrogant, she saw right through him. And she could tell him what to do because she knew him. Nancy gave slogans for players to remember such as "the proof is in the skating" or "get the most out of your game, get the most out of your body." She built them up emotionally for the ice and for later in life. She wanted players to be mentally tough and ready for anything on and off the ice.

"Power skating means each individual athlete getting the most of his body in order to work as efficiently as possible on the ice," said Mike. "It's tailor-made to each person. Get the most power out of your body for the longest time on the ice."

Mike learned from Nancy to isolate and work with his players individually (called "isolation training"), because everyone's physiology is different. Just like everyone can't wear the same pair of shoes, not everyone should be skating the same way. One player might have a deficit in his quadriceps or his hip flexors, so he should work those areas especially hard. Nancy taught Mike to analyze individual players from head to toe and find the weaknesses.

Players paid attention to Nancy as she preached perfection, and she gave rewards too. When a Roseau player got a hat trick (three goals in one game), Nancy personally delivered a hat to his house. This, and knowing how much she cared, inspired her players. Also, if a player had an injury, he would stop by the store for Nancy to massage a shoulder, leg, or neck.

"Nancy was a legend," Mike said. "What she started was phenomenal. She also influenced my career with her knowledge of massage and acupressure. I say on my resume that I've worked with Nancy Burggraf, and general managers and coaches know that her name carries respect throughout the entire hockey community."

9

Highway 11 – The War Road

*"You know what's in your head. If you want to think negatively,
that's your choice, but then you're going to play that way.
Keep your thoughts positive and realize the coach is trying to help you
by yelling at you sometimes. Keep things in perspective."*
—Nancy Burggraf's mental training sermon

March 1999

Before the boys got off the bus, Coach Bruce reminded them of
their two big wins that year against archrival Warroad. "That was the
best hockey I ever saw any Roseau team play," he told them. "Just play
the way you played in that first period against Warroad."

1999 (and every year since 1908)

For Nancy, the Rams players, coaches, and the entire community,
there was no bigger game day than when Roseau played Warroad at
Roseau Memorial Arena. Tension built throughout the day. Workers
cleaned snow and ice off the arena steps. Concession workers
prepped the hot dog and popcorn makers. It was a passionate rivalry
that extended beyond sports. Community spirit, pride, bragging
rights, and honor met at center ice.

Warroad, the reviled "W" word, the archrival on the shores of Lake
of the Woods, was 21 miles east across the bogs on Highway 11, the
actual war road that Sioux and Chippewa tribes used on their way to
battle. Known as Hockeytown, USA, Warroad has had a player on
every Olympic medal winning hockey team. For nearly a century, both
teams have slugged it out on the ice.

Months prior to the January 1999 game, Nancy was putting the Rams through their power skating paces and working on their mental game, reminding them to "explode out of the locker room and keep their game faces on."

Earlier that season, Roseau had beaten the Warriors in a hard-fought, close game. The last time the Rams won both games was in 1990, the same year the Rams won the state tournament. It made the old-timers and Nancy wonder, *Could a championship happen again?*

At Nelson's Café downtown, Roseau men met for coffee and pre-game chatter. "It depends on how the puck bounces," said one loyal Rams fan. "If we lose, the sun still comes up tomorrow, but it comes up in the east. And that means it comes up in Warroad first."

Two hours before the 7:30 p.m. face-off, Dell, retired farmer and former hockey player, and his wife Arlys found a spot on the green bench behind the Plexiglas window. It was a warm seat and had a perfect view of the visiting goal. Dell claims to be the first person to have skated on the ice at Roseau Arena, sneaking into the ice for a few minutes before his teammates suited up in 1949. He and his wife had watched their two sons and now would watch their two grandsons play hockey. "There's so much pressure on the kids," he said, admitting that passions could get a little carried away. "After all, they're not pros."

Roseau kept the pressure on Warroad in the early 1970s and 1980s, beating them for thirteen straight years. Some townspeople agreed about the intense pressure, saying it was like sending kids to the wolves. Others commented that it was about adults putting children on ice to accomplish something they didn't do when they were in high school. By 1999, the rivalry between Roseau and Warroad should have diminished a bit. Warroad, population 1,900, chose to stay in single A hockey, while Roseau, population 2,800, opted to play up against the bigger schools in Class AA. The two rivals would no longer meet in the state finals, since each class crowned their own champion. The rivals could no longer knock each other off before the state tournament. Both schools chose, however, to keep the local rivalry alive and played each other twice during the season.

And so, the rivalry had not diminished. Not a bit, in fact. As the sun set, 2,500 people packed the sold-out Roseau Arena. Fans calmed their pre-game jitters by drinking coffee. One fan commented, "It's like the fair coming to town. You get excited."

Neal Broten—Roseau native, 1980 Olympic gold medal winner with the "Miracle on Ice" team, former Minnesota North Star and New Jersey Devil Stanley Cup winner—showed up to sign autographs. Kids mobbed him. They all knew the legend of the greatest Roseau trio ever to play in Minnesota hockey during the mid 1970s, Neal Broten, his brother, Aaron Broten, and fellow lineman, Butsy Erickson.

At every home game, Broten's father, Newell, stood outside the boards on a ladder at the end of the rink where the Warroad goalie would be in the net for two of the three periods, and he turned on the red light when a Roseau player scored. He liked being able to watch Roseau attack for two periods and commented that he'd been doing this job for more than fifty years. During most arena hockey games, Nancy stood next to Newell, and her sharp whistle again and again during the game reminded players to focus and step up the quality of play. Players remembered that they could hear that whistle above everything else during a game.

By 7:30 p.m., the Rams Junior Varsity had wiped out the Warrior B squad. Two radio stations from each town broadcasted live as Bernie Burggraf gave colorful commentary of the Rams' play. Television stations from Grand Forks, North Dakota, provided live reports from the arena for regional viewers. The jammed building rocked with every seat full. The air electrified. The game was on.

The next day, the sun did rise in Warroad, but it did so to the trail of tears shed by Warroad fans on Highway 11 as they made their way home. Roseau skated to a 7-1 victory, scoring six of their goals right away in the first period. They had taken Nancy's advice to "explode on the ice" seriously. The paper reported that the Rams were on a mission of hope to reach the Target Center in Minneapolis and win the state championship.

In Nelson's Café, the mood was happy and light. Talk of the state tourney filled the air. Roseau was on top; life was good. The next day the *Grand Forks Herald* published an interview with the Warroad coach, Canadian-born Cary Eades. Cary said his team had played as if they had "five chairs and a goalie on the ice."

Ironically, when Cary Eades came from British Columbia to play Division I hockey at the University of North Dakota in 1978, he met his new power skating coach, who had trained him in strange methods that he christened "voodoo hockey." Her name was Nancy Burggraf.

Voodoo Hockey

*"Now, you can have edges so you can turn on a dime
and give nine cents change." —Nancy Burggraf*

March 1999

On Thursday afternoon, Roseau met Rochester Mayo in the first
State Tournament game. At the Roseau Hospital, Bernie and Nancy
turned on the television for game-day coverage.

1980s–1990s

By the late 1970s, Minnesota, North Dakota, and South Dakota
towns throughout the region had seen the benefit of Nancy's camps
and clinics with Roseau players, and they wanted in on the action.
With Bernie's help in promoting the clinics, Nancy began traveling in
North Dakota to Fargo, Minot, Bismarck, Grafton, Williston, and Valley
City; to Huron, Aberdeen, and Watertown in South Dakota; and to St.
Cloud, Moorhead, Detroit Lakes, Fergus Falls, Thief River Falls,
Worthington, and Richfield in Minnesota. All the while, she continued
to work at the store and her training sessions at the arena.

Rube Bjorkman

Another man was about to open hockey doors for Nancy, and
once again she took full advantage. Two-time Olympian Rube

Bjorkman, Bergetta's half-brother and Nancy's uncle, had played at UND as the "Masked Marvel" in the 1940s. He grew up in Roseau but coached and taught math in Coleraine, Minnesota, after finishing college. Then the University of New Hampshire hired him as head hockey coach where he stayed from 1964 to 1968 and was named Division II Coach of the Year in 1968.

Rube grew up playing outdoor hockey in Northern Minnesota winters. It could be downright painful at times at 30–40 degrees below zero and a 15-mph north wind. He remembered that at those frigid temperatures, pucks often shattered when they hit the goal post. Local sports writers wrote that Rube was blessed with everything: a smooth skating style, speed, agility, soft hands, great stick handling, and intelligence. But he lacked great eyesight. Forced to wear goggle-type glasses, Rube looked like he was wearing a mask. Fans dubbed him the "Masked Marvel," and the nickname stuck even after he replaced his glasses with contact lenses. Rube and Nancy's brother Bob led Roseau to their first Minnesota State High School championship in 1946. Both men went on to play for the University of Minnesota, and Rube also played in the 1948 Olympic Games in Switzerland and the 1952 games in Norway.

Rube had attended the skating extravaganzas his niece Nancy produced, and he observed how her power skating instruction produced some of the finest skaters in Minnesota. From 1968 to 1978, Rube coached at UND and later became president of the American College Hockey Coaches Association. Rube had been working at hockey schools around Minnesota, and it became obvious to him that UND needed to begin summer hockey camps for younger players. In all the camps he had attended, no one had created a program like Nancy's "power skating." He thought it would be a good addition, something unique to draw players to the UND camp. He immediately thought of Nancy, who agreed to the challenge and began a long tradition of power skating sessions at the University of North Dakota.

Dean Blais

After being head coach at Roseau High School and then assistant at UND, Dean Blais became head coach at UND after Gino Gasparini

left in 1994 to become Commissioner for the United States Hockey League. "Nancy was our biggest selling point at UND Hockey School," Dean said. "It was a great school with more ice time, but the big thing was Nancy Burggraf's power skating instruction. She touched the lives of hundreds of kids." He was so impressed with Nancy and her techniques that he decided to ask her to help with the Varsity team.

During one season, Nancy worked with Jay Caufield, who had never played hockey before coming to UND. Jay arrived at UND excited to play football, but when he hurt his neck, he was no longer allowed to play football. So he went out for hockey. After two years of UND Sioux hockey and Burggraf training, Jay ended up playing for the Pittsburgh Penguins, who won the Stanley Cup twice in the early 1990s. He credited Nancy's program with improving his skills more so than any other aspect of the game.

"Nancy was easygoing off the ice," Dean commented, "but when she was on the ice, she did it her way. I mean, you absolutely had to follow her directions and do what she told you to do. She took groups of campers, about forty 11- and 12-year-olds and had them regimented. She worked on about 25 different skills daily and the players did it. No question. They respected her. Off the ice, personally, she was like a member of my family."

During UND games, Dean gave Nancy and Bernie access to the secured players' area downstairs. During one game Nancy ran down between periods to tell the person who sharpened skates to check the radius. The Sioux were skating uphill with too much blade on the ice. She could tell this by watching their acceleration and noticing that their feet were not quick enough. She advocated the hollow grind in sharpening skates, which required a special stone so the player's skate was sharpened on both edges, inner and outer. When a player turned, the skate would "bite" the ice. If a player lost an edge, *pow*!, he'd start to slide.

During one game against the University of Minnesota, Duluth, Nancy noticed that the Bulldogs locked their sticks underneath the Sioux sticks so UND couldn't get them down to deflect the puck.

"Bernie," said Nancy, "go down and tell Dean." So Bernie ran down to Dean who made sure the guys went in with their sticks on the ice so they could get the deflections. Many deflections later, UND won the game.

The couple debriefed every game as they drove back to Roseau from UND, talking about what each team or player could have done, reveling in or pitying what they did do. "Isn't this a beautiful game?" Nancy said to Bernie on one of the drives. "Like basketball . . . pass, break, and use your speed."

Dean credits Nancy with UND's success as one of the best skating teams in the country and winners of four national championships since 1980. Nancy helped them with quickness, mobility, endurance, starting, stopping, and balance. He learned, however, that Nancy's hockey abilities were an extension of the total person, and he felt that Nancy really knew people. She cared about each skater she coached and was disappointed if someone didn't work up to his or her potential.

Cary Eades

Over Cary's four years at UND, Nancy helped the team win two NCAA titles. He said that her "voodoo hockey" combined skating knowledge with an understanding of the human body and the spirit of the sport. She put players through drills some only dimly comprehended, drills many couldn't finish. She used acupressure and reflexology to ease player's pains.

"She was ahead of her time," Cary said, "with her techniques and drills and her teaching about being in the zone, being mentally ready, the psychology of the game, and weightlifting. In those days, women working with macho hockey players just wasn't done. And there were some guys that had big problems with a woman doing this. She got us into yoga and stretching too. We thought it was a little bizarre, and some of the drills were strange, but it worked. Nancy was intense, businesslike, demanding, and focused. Players quickly realized that she knew her stuff because their skating improved."

When Cary worked at the hockey schools with Nancy, she often used him as an example of the wrong way—to show people how they shouldn't skate—because he had a very short stride. "She was in your

face, but had an arm around you at the same time," reflected Cary. "She was a classy lady who had to get on me sometimes and say, 'Quit messing around, young man. Let's get to business.'"

On training breaks, Nancy played cards and cribbage with the players. She was always comfortable around the guys and very focused on the games. She liked to win everything; in card games, they played for popsicles. On one hand, she comforted young players at the camp if they were homesick. On the other hand, she took the game and the program seriously. The diminutive Nancy once lowered a college player to the ice and said, "I'm not here to babysit you. Get to work."

Craig Ludwig

In the mid-1970s, big and powerful Craig Ludwig arrived at UND. A burly defenseman, he couldn't skate backward fast enough during games. Day after day Nancy skated with him, virtually carrying him as he learned the art and physics of moving backward on blades. Later he went on to a 17-year career in the NHL, and when Nancy met Craig's father, he put his arms around her and said, "He owes it all to you."

UND players came to Nancy for additional pointers and motivation. Before games, several players brought Nancy their sticks. She made a fist, stood the sticks on end, and pounded them.

"What's she doing?" asked another player.

"She's pounding goals into our sticks."

He laughed.

He was quickly rebuffed. "Don't laugh. It works."

Within minutes, the player who had laughed handed his stick to Nancy.

Nancy convinced players to believe in themselves. "How you practice is how you will play," she hollered at them to energize them. Some players she confronted head on. One particular young UND player had tremendous "jets" on the ice. He could really move, and Nancy saw his potential. But his attitude was suffering. After a power skating session, she took him off in the corner.

"Listen," she said looking at him eye to eye. "Now that we've worked on your skating and your stick handling, we have to work on your personality. Don't be so 'itchy' in the locker room that the guys hate ya. They won't ever give ya the puck."

She was able to talk to guys like that—and they took it and changed.

Mike Commodore

UND and NHL player Mike Commodore remembers Nancy as looking organized and neat. The first time he saw her, during his freshman year, skating around on the rink, he asked himself, "What's with the little old lady? What the heck is goin' on here?" Then she started bringing in all these drills, and he fell all over the place. "Basically," he said, "she taught me how to skate. If she said it was going to be an easy day, we'd usually go out there and after fifteen minutes we couldn't skate anymore—we were just dead with our tongues hanging out." The next day, Nancy would promise the players a hard day and they would let out a collective groan. They couldn't move their legs from the day before. And sure enough, Nancy would smile and give them an easy day.

Scott Sandlin

A native of Hibbing, Minnesota, Scott Sandlin played for UND from 1982 until 1986 and then played professionally six years for Montreal, Philadelphia, and Minnesota. He went on to become the head coach at University of Minnesota-Duluth. He remembers spending time with Nancy and doing power skating drills in the summers and during night sessions. "Nancy would take me out on the ice," he said, "and make me skate to this funky music, sometimes Neil Diamond, sometimes classical. She gave me her business card; I still carry it. She wrote on the back 'stride out' and that was one thing she always worked on with me. She'd blare that music over the speakers at UND, and for twenty minutes we'd just skate around and around. She kept telling us, 'Stride out, stride out, stride out.'"

Many players like Scott felt embarrassed at first because they couldn't do some of the drills that this 50-year-old woman could do. At the same time, they appreciated her innovative approach and repetition that forced them to learn the finesse and techniques of skating. One player said she turned them into "dragon flies" on ice, flitting and darting everywhere with great quickness. They buzzed out there because they had confidence in their skating. In another instance, a 6'5" player smarted off to Nancy one day during a clinic. She grabbed him, pulled him toward her, and said, "Start skating or get out. This isn't a daycare center."

Red-faced, the guy, too embarrassed to approach Nancy, skated over to Frank, who was assisting his mother that day. "Sorry," he said. Frank retorted, "Don't say sorry to me, say sorry to her. Start skatin' or go home." It didn't matter how big the players were, Nancy was not afraid to be strict with her training regimen.

It also didn't matter if you were a professional skater or a Squirt, Nancy gave the same treatment. If a player pulled his weight, that was good enough; but if he slacked off, she'd tell him to shape up or leave the ice. Nancy wasn't about to let anyone waste her time. She gave 100 percent and she expected that in return.

Other coaches were "compelled" by her methods like the ankle-building exercise, where skaters had to propel themselves down the ice on one skate and then turn around and come back on the other one. It prevented the ankles from caving inward. Nancy also had players put their arms out with hands straightforward balancing a puck on each hand. The idea was to skate from the hips down with the upper body motionless while not giving up their stride. Players dropped the pucks two or three times and had to pick them back up, only to lose them two or three more times. It sometimes took two years of practice before players could finally accomplish that drill at camp.

Players tried to convince Nancy to play "harder" rock-and-roll music during warm-ups, but she never put it on because she thought it would drive the players nuts. She thought classical and Neil Diamond tunes relaxed players and got them in the right frame of mind while stretching.

Burggrafs on Ice

Nancy's discipline carried over to her sons. Frank skated at UND from 1978 to 1982, and he distinctly remembered her whistle, the same one she had used to call the kids in at night when he was a boy. The whistle had different tones; it had its own language. He said the shrill sound inspired him to skate a little harder.

Frank skated on the 1980 NCAA championship team while Charlie skated on a WCHA championship and NCAA runner-up team. Oldest son Rick played for the Roseau High School team and went on to UND with a hockey scholarship but quit his sophomore year. A self-proclaimed "horrid" skater, Rick felt he matured late; as a boy he was a skinny little ragamuffin who always got hurt in hockey. By college he had broken both arms, cracked a rib and a jaw, and had rheumatic fever. Rick joked that Bernie took out extra insurance to make money on his injuries.

Scouts from across the country on both the collegiate and professional levels attended Nancy's clinics. She was big on helping the smaller skaters who fell through the cracks of hockey heaven—a fighter, a do-er, and an advocate of the kids who got lost in the shuffle. "So many kids don't play for winning teams," she said, "but are good hockey players if given the chance."

Nancy kept a small notebook, a manual of all her drills and techniques, where she used her own language and made notations taken from aerobatics airplane sign language to show the direction of the drills. One day at a UND power skating session, she set down her notebook on the bleachers to demonstrate a "shoot the duck" move for the players. When she returned to retrieve her manual, it was gone. It had been her only copy. Nancy really didn't care; she had it all in her head and could make another copy. But Frank was livid; he knew someone from a national hockey organization had been watching from the bleachers that day. Frank believed that person purposely came to steal Nancy's techniques. One year later, that same organization came out with a similar training program, changed just slightly, but obvious to the family that it was Nancy's methods. Once again, Nancy was not bothered, but Frank starting pushing for his mother to make a video of her techniques. At first she wanted nothing

to do with the idea because her time was already filled with camps and clinics.

Confiding in her daughter Becky, Nancy said she felt sad that the town of Roseau didn't seem to support her in her power skating as much as the other towns where she conducted clinics. Becky thought at the time that some in Roseau were just jealous, that they did not want her to succeed and resented her making money from hockey clinics. "My mom was very sensitive to others," said Nancy's youngest daughter Cook. "She often told me she wore her heart on her sleeve. She never wanted to miss an opportunity to have somebody know that it wasn't just your outside edge/inside edge, it's your heart and your faith too."

Becky thought it was hard on her mother not getting the recognition she deserved in her hometown. "She had such a gift for being able to look at a player and tell where the problems were," said Becky. "It could be very elementary, the way a muscle group wasn't strong enough, or just the basics like keeping your stick down and your head up, bending your knees, sitting back a little bit—just those kinds of fine tuning."

In Becky's estimation, some men in the coaching ranks felt intimidated that her mom really did know what she was doing and what she was talking about. "I think they found it hard that a woman could do all this, and as a result some of the jealousy made it difficult for her."

At first, even Nancy's brother Bob wondered, "What is Nancy doing? She doesn't know about hockey. She's never even played." He kept that attitude until he attended a Detroit Red Wings game and saw them using Burggraf drills and techniques. He became a believer.

Throughout the years there were detractors, but Nancy chose not to go head-to-head with them. She just continued to teach people how to skate. And the momentum became so great that the dissenting voices diminished, and she became more and more popular with coaches outside the area. At one time people asked the Burggraf children, "Are you related to the Burggrafs who played at UND?" Ten years later the question had changed to, "Are you related to Nancy Burggraf?"

ISO is born

Following college graduation from UND, Frank and Rick continued to help Nancy run the clinics, the official name of which became Burggraf Skating Skills. They worked to hone the Burggraf techniques of breaking down the skating game for the different aspects of speed, power, acceleration, balance, and agility. Frank and Nancy both saw the need to take her clinics to another level when they witnessed a prominent college coach from another camp filling out the skaters' evaluations in a training room. The coach said he was too busy (he was playing cribbage), so he had his 12-year-old son fill out the evaluations for campers with statements such as "much improved," "good job," "see you next year." And the coach signed his name. Nancy turned to Frank, "That's just wrong. Let's keep giving people the most we can for their dollar. Let's develop a new mission for our program."

That day, the unique ISO was born. Burggraf ISOlation clinics introduced a new philosophy: isolate each player's needs in terms of strength and hockey skills and work with more skaters as individuals with individual training programs. At this point Nancy agreed to make a video in order to take the training to a new level. "We knew," said Frank, "that if we made a manual and a video, Burggraf trade secrets would be out." Nancy replied to this, "Well, it's going to make the game better. It's time other people learn how to do this." The duo wrote the manual at a level that the kids, parents, and coaches could understand, and outlined a system that they could follow.

"Hockey camps aren't what they once were," said Nancy in a newspaper interview. "A few years ago, they really did help a kid's skills improve, and the kid worked hard through the summer. Now, they're for kids whose parents drop them off for two weeks and use the camps as a babysitting service. The camps have lost their meaning, and that's why I wanted to develop the ISO clinic—because I'm committed to developing excellence."

After Burggraf ISO clinics, players were rated on stride, transition skating, balance, agility, flexibility, speed, power, acceleration, and endurance. Goalies were rated on body control, stance, net orientation

skills, overall leg strength, and lateral mobility. Points ranging from "below average" to "excellent" were also given for the obstacle course, puck handling, and shooting skills. Following the clinic, Nancy presented a report card to skaters with her comments and areas for each player to concentrate on. She never stopped thinking about ways to improve her skills presentation and how to develop programs to help hockey players get the attention they deserved from college and pro teams.

Stick Down, Head Up, the video and manual published in 1990, became a benchmark for various hockey programs. In the game of hockey, little information innovation flows north across the border into Canada. But the Burggraf video sold better in Canada than in the United States. "It's their game," Frank said. "To them this training is pure gold; it's worth something." Besides the Canadian Amateur Hockey Association, the Chicago Blackhawks, Dallas Stars, New York Islanders, and the New Jersey Devils also purchased videos.

"We probably gave away more videos than we sold," said Frank. "My mom didn't like the exposure or like to advertise. She kept saying, 'We're in this for the puck, not the buck.'"

It wasn't a glamorous life. One night Frank and Nancy were running a clinic in Devil's Lake, North Dakota, in an arena with natural ice and no heat. It was forty below zero, and the Burggrafs had to change in a warming room where the Zamboni was parked. A big water heater stood in the corner where Frank and Nancy took turns hugging it for warmth. Frank's job was to blow the whistle so the skaters would stop between drills. He finally just stood hugging the water heater blowing the whistle randomly. He kept blowing and blowing until finally Nancy approached; the clinic was over. "Are you done yet?" she asked.

Over the years, as the Burggraf clinics grew in popularity, Frank estimated that Nancy and her assistant coaches were on the ice teaching for six days a week in the summer months. In the winter, Nancy and company traveled throughout the upper Midwest and her sons remembered nearly fifty nights in small North Dakota towns where they had to beg their mom to get off the ice. They had a hard time matching her stamina.

All the while, Nancy kept her life colorful. She drove a red cherry Mustang with white leather seats, and her love for speed led her to become good friends with the Minnesota Highway Patrol officers that covered Highway 11 as she drove to hockey clinics in the region.

Power Skating Philosophy

At first, coaches at all levels of hockey thought that power skating meant skating up and down the ice about 40 or 50 times until a player got fatigued. Then, Nancy began to refer to "recovery" from fatigue and how to avoid cheating on stride. Some players, who might be stronger on one leg, tended to use that particular leg more when tired. "You need to stride out equally on both legs," Nancy pointed out at her clinics. "Your recovery time becomes important so you can keep going stronger and keep consistency in your stride."

Parents who watched Nancy work were amazed that she could turn her back on the players and no one screwed around (firing random pucks) but just paid attention. Players knew her reputation and how well respected she was in power skating since the 1970s. Coaches credited Nancy and her legacy for helping focus on the two- to three-week period at the start of the season when teams work on strength building and power skating drills. More acceleration programs have sprung up across the country because of Nancy's innovative methods.

Eventually, traveling from town to town exhausted Nancy, and her goal was to have clinics centrally located so that everyone could come to her. She and family members decided on the Moorhead Sports Center where they rented ice time and a room upstairs for weights and off-ice training. Professional as well as high school and younger players came to Moorhead for a two-week August summer camp with an optional one-week pre-camp "add on." The number of players attending is limited based on the number of available coaches; the goal is for players to get the individual attention they need. By the late 1990s, Burggraf ISO and Skating Skills had trained over 150 NHL players and even more Division I, II, and III hockey players from across the United States and Canada, adding up to more than 40,000 skaters in all her five decades of training.

At Burggraf ISO, players put in long days, starting with an early morning, warm-up stretches with a trainer, and drills at several "stations" across the ice all morning, and a couple welcome breaks when the Zamboni came on to clean the ice. In the afternoon, players worked individualized weight programs and plyometrics, and they scrimmaged at night. The pros appreciated the chance to get in great shape and felt like they skated better right before they started their seasons. Some said it was like boot camp. Besides dry-land training, drills, and evening scrimmages, Burggraf Isolation Hockey Clinics also involved videotaping each player to help in review and critique of the player's progress. One eight-year veteran coach, trained by Frank Burggraf in the ISO techniques, noted that many players attending had been sent by their NHL agents to help improve their skating and worth in the market.

This coach recalled an incident between Nancy and an NHL player early one morning at the camp. Nancy was directing a pre-skate stretch while players skated to classical music. They formed six lines at the goal line and came out in waves of six players as the previous groups got halfway down the ice. Players were skating all over the rink, doing leg kick-ups and groin stretches under Nancy's watchful eye, when a tall NHL pro cracked his stick over a goalie's helmet after the goalie made a snide comment. The goalie shook it off and whirled around to break his stick across the other player's back. They started slugging it out. Nancy closed in. She wedged herself between the two skaters, separated them, and proceeded to chew them out. Later Nancy learned that the two guys had exchanged blows during the scrimmage the night before. People watching said it was a surreal drama on ice set to classical music with a small older woman out-maneuvering two large hockey players.

11

The Wounded Healer

"I feel as though I'm sinking into darkness. I want to learn more and know more. My desire is to matter, to count in life."
—*Nancy's journal, 1998*

March 4, 1999

Game 1: Roseau Rams vs. Rochester Mayo Spartans
The Minnesota State High School Hockey Tournament
The TV announcer began:

At 3:34 into the first period, Rams player Mike Klema scores his 22nd goal of the season and at 8 minutes into the second period, David Klema scores his 15th.

It's the third and final period and getting down to the nitty gritty for the Rams, decked out in their school colors green and white. The Rams enter the final period leading 2-0. When it looks like the Rams couldn't lose, a Mayo kid, Canzello, unloads one from the top of the circle. It flies past the side stick of Jake Brandt and the score is 2-1. The Mayo fans find their vocal chords. Their prayers to slow down Roseau may be answered.

With 3:30 left in the contest, a Mayo kid, Sam Everson, catches Brandt by surprise. With a quick wrist shot, he drills it past Jake. Score: 2-2. The Mayo fans are deafening. This game is about momentum.

Nineteen seconds later the Rams' "Big O," Josh Olson, lets loose a high wrist shot at the 2:44 mark. It's Josh's 20th goal of the season. The Rams ice the win with an open net goal by Mike Klema with three seconds remaining. Rams 4, Mayo 2.

"To me, the victory was never in doubt," said Bernie, who called his Rams the "Jolly Green Giants" of the game. With glistening eyes and after two sleepless nights excited in the hospital, Nancy raised her thumb in agreement.

Next up, The Holy Angels Stars.

1990s

Nancy used all her gifts, rarely saying no when she thought she could be of service. Outside the community of Roseau, her hockey reputation increased. In Roseau, however, other people talked behind her back. "Shouldn't Nancy be spending more time at home? . . . Where does she go for those long weekends? . . . What about her husband and family?"

"I had no idea what she was doing for the world of hockey," said Nancy's good friend Eleanor Johnson. "I couldn't believe it when she told me how huge the clinics had become and how much in demand she was. No one in Roseau really knew all that was going on."

The powerful men in Minnesota hockey saw Nancy's success with her clinics and accused her of milking the system for personal gain partially because their turf was being threatened. But why shouldn't Nancy have enjoyed some financial success from using her gifts, just as men had done in the hockey world before her? She was treading on the politics of Minnesota hockey. She knew it but quietly kept going.

Through the store, Nancy continued to bring a sense of style to Roseau, but this style led to perfectionism in the store and in her own image. "Everything had to be perfect for my mom," said Becky. "She had to look perfect even in jeans and a sweatshirt. Perfectly tailored. She might only wear an outfit once and throw it. Yes, throw it in the garbage because she didn't like it anymore. I tried to be there when she tossed the clothes because we were the same size and I loved her style."

Nancy's perfectionism and eagerness to please others drove her to clean like a cyclone at home and become a precise technician of the game of hockey on ice. This drive shadowed her life. Questioning the meaning of her life, Nancy wrote in 1984, "Maybe one can't work oneself to death, but to tears is a sure thing—sometimes it seems so pointless."

"I remember coming to Nancy's house for coffee," said Eleanor. "She never sat down. Not once. She was cleaning all the time—wiping the counter, sweeping the floor, dusting, and taking sips of coffee in between. Tidying up the house had been her responsibility as a young girl, and she never stopped, I guess. She took her cleaning seriously."

Nancy also sought to be perfect in her faith, and she continually pursued an understanding of God, which came from a deep desire for validation.

"All that my mom did came at a price," said Rick. "I felt I had to share my mom with the world. Our family sacrificed and sacrificed. Believe me, when my mom set her mind to doing something, it was done. But at a price."

"Mom was out to prove herself," said Charlie. "She was a wounded healer who loved to help people. She got right in the middle of their lives."

Charlie thought his mom felt a need to suffer in order to learn how to be a servant to others. It gave her empathy for their hurting. He remembered sitting with his mom by a campfire where she made a list of all who had hurt her, prayed, and then threw the list in the fire. "Roseau can be a provincial place," he said. "Some in Roseau thought, 'Who does Nancy think she is?'" Charlie likens Nancy to Belle in *Beauty and the Beast*. They told Belle to put her books down; she wasn't allowed to read or learn. The hockey powers and some in Roseau told Nancy to stop teaching. But she didn't. She wanted to know herself and use her gifts. But she did it in a quiet way without needing rewards, and now thousands of kids know her. She had a quiet ministry of skating, and it didn't matter if her students would ever turn pro or not.

Nancy also believed that she had the gift of physical healing. Her life was all about the power of physical touch combined with prayer,

and she wanted to use her "praying thumbs." She met and prayed with individuals who were ill; news of this spread by word of mouth. Doctors from the Roseau hospital sometimes requested that Nancy visit terminally ill patients to offer massage and acupressure. Bernie called this "Nancy's labor of love," and it surprised him when the MDs started calling.

One day, Nancy had been at the hospital visiting seriously ill patients, giving them back rubs, foot rubs, acupressure, and praying with them. Nancy called her friend and asked her to come to the hospital, "Eleanor, you'll be praying while I work my thumbs."

When one of the patients' blood pressure improved drastically after Nancy's massage, she reported the results to Eleanor and then headed for Messiah Lutheran Church and rang the church bell to celebrate just like she always did for her patients who improved.

Rev. Lou Hermanson, the pastor at Messiah, remarked, "I always wondered why that bell would go off at odd times."

Lou believed that in another time, Nancy would have been a pastor. "Nancy had a strong feeling that God wanted her to do mission work. She struggled to understand God's will in her life. She asked, 'Have I done something worthwhile with my life? Am I productive? Am I a faithful witness?' She looked for signs that what she was doing was right in God's eyes."

Nancy, who had tried hard to please her own father, now sought to please her heavenly father. In all of Lou's years in Roseau, Nancy worked to heal others. Intuitively she knew the places in the body for healing. Even a gifted healer learns, however, that there are limits to the power, and it grieved Nancy that when her mother had cancer, she couldn't do anything to help her. Nancy said she wanted to conquer the big C. Though remorseful that she was unable to do more for her mom, Nancy was not afraid to bathe, wash, and touch Bergetta. Nancy didn't stand at a distance. She would lie in bed with her mother, which was a very touching scene for Lou.

Nancy also underlined her Bible from beginning to end. She brought in works by the great theologians for Lou's interpretation and kept him on his toes theologically. She was interested in the gifts of the spirit. "We would talk sometimes four or five hours, about having faith as small as a mustard seed," said Lou. "She was very concerned her faith wasn't strong enough. I told her not to worry. The concern itself was a sign that she was a person of faith."

Lou and Nancy talked in terms of why things turn out the way they do, and obviously there were no easy answers.

"Nancy wanted to take care of people, both mind and body," said Lou, "to put them at peace with the world, with themselves, with families. She was very interested in the idea of hospice."

Nancy was not afraid to touch people because she believed hurting people needed touching. Nancy touched and prayed, hoping she could heal or, if nothing else, bring a deep peace. Some mornings Nancy would wake up about 5 a.m., feeling "so full of God." She prayed and asked what God wanted her to do that day. By seven o'clock, her already full day of the store and hockey would be booked with sick and injured people who wanted her to visit. When Nancy visited, she prayed, shared scripture readings, and took her little bottle of healing oil. When a friend called her for something social, she often replied, "I can't today, I'm serving."

Nancy's healing hands mended hockey wounds as well. "I had plenty of cuts on my face from hockey," said Frank, "and mom would clean the cut and hold it together with her fingers for a half an hour. I never had a scar." She also helped Frank's shoulder when it was separated after a game so the swelling went down faster and he could play the next day. She worked acupressure miracles on players' knees and ankles so they could get back on the ice quicker. Frank said Nancy could help headaches, hiccups, and sinus trouble by massaging players' hands and the backs of their necks.

At age 57, Nancy still found herself searching for God's calling in her life. The continual hockey clinics were grueling, and in her journals she wrote that they became very repetitious and it was good that players changed from clinic to clinic. Working at the store tired her out, and she felt her true talents were not being used. She also wanted to study and learn more about the human body. Nancy consulted Lou about her interest in the ambulance squad.

"Would I make a good EMT?" she asked Lou, who was also on the squad.

"Of course I encouraged her," he recalls.

Nancy became certified and a bit nervous about her first ambulance run. "You always wonder how you'll do," Lou said. "But Nancy was even-tempered, compassionate, and an eager learner."

When Nancy was out of town, she rode along with other ambulance services to learn what she could from them. She brought certificates from other places, such as Minnesota or North Dakota towns where she ran clinic and camps, to show she had been taking extra EMT classes. Nancy had the ability to stay calm under stressful situations and was on call whenever possible. She would leave everything and come.

One day, as Nancy worked in the store, one car broadsided another near the Ben Franklin Store on Main Street. An elderly man, Rueben, had had a stroke while driving and lost control of his vehicle. Nancy called an ambulance, ran out of the store, opened the car door, and cradled Rueben's head in her arms. She knew from his vital signs, appearance, and breathing that he was likely dying.

"Oh, it's you, Nancy," Rueben said. "I'm so glad it's you." And he lost consciousness. She told him, "Rueben, you are going to be with Pearl." His wife had died a few years before.

Nancy rode in the ambulance with him and stayed at his family's side until he died later that day.

In June of 1990, Nancy reported having a good day in her journals with hardworking groups at her hockey clinics and responsible counselors. She also reported an EMT day that was wild, with way too much trauma to record. "I'm praying that I'm where God wants me to be," she wrote.

Nancy continued, however, to work on developing an inner peace. Hockey clinics did not always go as planned. "Bad camp day," she wrote. " First counselor overslept the first three hours so guys missed out. Another guy late so shirts locked up. But I've changed to no longer huff and puff and it works out. I'm glad God provides inner peace."

At a UND summer hockey camp, Nancy reported, "Last drill day. Thinking of the end! It gets pretty lonely sometimes—lots of acupressure today—kid went into terrible asthma attack—I pressured it away—he thought it was a miracle. Perhaps! Cuz the thumbs were praying—always!"

Nancy began to develop her own battle wounds She reported weekly and sometimes daily episodes of "jump chest," or heart palpitations. She tried to control them with breathing, yoga, and acupressure. In 1993, she broke her wrist during an instruction clinic in Minneapolis when a rut in the ice sent her crashing.

"I didn't know anyone who could take me to the hospital," Nancy said in a newspaper interview. "So I put up with the pain for the rest of the session and until the next day when I flew home. I have to wear a cast for a while, but it won't slow me down, and I expect to maintain my schedule." More serious shadows, however, began to appear in her health in 1997.

Valley of the Shadow

"I'm searching so hard. I'm searching for strength and joy.
I'm failing to find it. I want my voice back.
The refs ignored too much stick work in the Roseau game."
—Nancy Burggraf journal, 1997

March 5, 1999

Game 2: Roseau Rams vs. Holy Angels Stars
The Minnesota State High School Hockey Tournament

Next up, Holy Angels Stars. At 7:05 p.m. on Friday, Bernie turned on the hospital TV.

It's the local boys versus the "open enrollment" boys. Holy Angels has six players from the Bloomington Jefferson program. It's how things are done in the big city where the kids change schools more often than they change caps. The Roseau motto of the night: Have stick, will travel!

The Stars can't contain Mike Klema, who scores not just a hat trick but added one more for good measure. Thirty-three seconds into the contest, Mike grabs a loose puck and drills it into the net. Forty-five seconds later, Phil Larson grabs another loose puck and shoots it over the goalie's right shoulder. Rams lead 2-0.

Mike scores his second goal on an empty net for a 3-0 lead. One minute into the second period and Matt Erickson backhands the puck to shoot the Rams into a 4-0 lead. Eighteen seconds later, the Stars get on the scoreboard with a shot fired from the bottom of the circle, and they put the puck in between Jake's pads. Score 4-1.

Mike scores his hat trick at 10:56. Rams lead 5-1. Off a face-off, one more puck slips by Jake at 12:51. In the third period, Mike takes a feed from Jesse Modahl and drills a high slap shot over the goalie. Final score: 6-2 Rams, and a berth in the state championship.

"Well, Holy Angels gave up the ghost," said Bernie, smiling. Nancy lifted her thumb.

Late 1990s

Nancy noticed that in the summer of 1997 her speech began to slur, and she prayed for her own healing while working in the store and keeping up with her clinics, EMT calls, and acupressure treatments for others. But it was eating her. Why couldn't she help heal herself? Friends asked, "What's wrong with Nancy?" At her 45-year class reunion in the summer, Nancy communicated through Bernie because he was still able to understand her slurring speech. Frustrated, Nancy found no answers from prayers or doctors. One Roseau resident made a snide comment that he thought "Nancy's best friend had become Jack Daniels."

In her 1997 journal she wrote, "Holy Spirit, Truth Divine, Dawn upon this soul of mine. Work of God and inward light, wake my spirit, clear my sight."

"Got a leather jacket today from the Sioux," she continued to write. "Has my name on it with the fighting Sioux emblem. Nice. My body is so stiff. Wish my voice was ok. Body doesn't feel right. Help God! I want to know what's wrong with me. How it can be fixed. I don't much like me. Help! Help! Help!"

Nancy read a newspaper article where Dean (Blais) said how he loved the way Nancy challenged players, how she helped increase their speed, acceleration, and balance in the off-season. But in her journal, she drew a cartoon character depicting herself as an old crow on ice.

For an upcoming Sioux clinic, Nancy asked her grandson, Mike (Becky's son), a sophomore at UND, to help her out at Engelstad Arena with the training. Because her voice had become so weak, Nancy wrote down the drills the players needed to do, and Mike carried them out for her. It wasn't his first time helping "Nana" (what the grandkids called her), but it was a slow process with her not being able to speak. Mike watched as Sioux after Sioux hockey player came up to Nancy and said how much they had missed her. Towering over Nancy, each player stooped down to give her a hug. Her smile and thumbs-up let the players know it was their Nancy. Unknown to Mike and Nancy, this was to be her last power skating clinic with the Sioux.

As Mike waited for Nancy to prepare a drill, he recalled his first time on skates when his Uncle Frank put him, at age three, on the ice. When he got older, he often helped Nancy during the summer UND clinic where he'd practiced her drills along with the Sioux. Whenever Nancy cranked up her warm-up music, Mike smiled, as he'd hear "Cracklin' Rosie" or "Forever in Blue Jeans." He grew strangely fond of Neil Diamond and wondered, how could the players get so pumped up to "Sweet Caroline"?

Every morning before Mike helped Nancy on the ice, they would do two things. First they would pray to "put on the full armor of the Lord" to protect them through the day, and then they had a chewable vitamin C tablet together. Mike's friends never quite understood why he enjoyed spending summers with his grandma, but who wouldn't want to hang out with all the big names in Sioux hockey? Plus, there weren't many young guys whose grandma drove a cherry red Mustang convertible either.

Mike got to know his grandmother's quiet side as well. During his times with her, they played cribbage for chocolate, took walks, or just relaxed. Mike knew Nancy loved all her grandchildren, but his special bond with her was through hockey.

As Nancy finished writing her drills for Mike, she headed out with him to be on the ice with the Sioux. After two hours on the ice, they watched the team's normal practice. When they finished, Nancy took Mike back to his dorm room.

"I love you, Nana, and I'm so proud of you," said Mike as he hugged Nancy.

Nancy took off her green and white leather Sioux jacket and handed it to Mike.

She wrote on her notepad, "It would be really cool for you to have this. I'm not going to need it anymore."

"Nana, that's your jacket. I can't take your jacket. You'll still need it when you help the Sioux again." Mike handed the jacket back to Nancy.

In her 1997 journal, Nancy often noted dizziness and a lack of energy. She even fainted a few times. Her local doctor gave her medicine for ulcers and depression, thinking the stress of her mother's death two years earlier might be causing her physical illness. In August, doctors "scoped" her throat hoping to find answers. None came.

On September 17, 1997, Nancy and Bernie drove to the Mayo Clinic in Rochester, Minnesota, for more tests. Nancy said she prayed her way through the tests. Pastor Lou sent her off to Mayo with a reminder that even faith "as small as a mustard seed" is good enough for God.

The doctors at Mayo found nothing conclusive in their testing. They suggested to Nancy that she see a psychiatrist. Furious, Nancy couldn't talk back, but she stomped out of the doctor's office. She knew it wasn't a psychological problem; something was wrong with her body. She did wonder, however, whether Bergetta's death might have triggered this physical response, causing her slurred speech? She missed her mother, especially in these moments of weakness. Nancy bought a book by theologian C. S. Lewis on grief, hoping it would give her insight into her physical symptoms and her mother's death.

Back in the fall of 1995, as Bergetta's cancer had worsened, Nancy kept up a fast pace during the peak of hockey clinics. Bergetta had surgery and began chemotherapy. Committed to keeping Bergetta at home, Nancy met with hospice staff. "My mom wants to stay home," she told them. "I will do everything I can to help her." Nancy wrote about how difficult it was for her to see her mom suffering. From her bed, however, Bergetta still managed to watch hockey games, and she frowned and shook her head when the refs made a bad call.

Nancy, affected physically with increased bouts of heart palpitations, struggled to keep up her own energy.

On Christmas Day 1995, Nancy got up early to put a turkey in the oven. Rick and Cook's families came over to open presents. When Becky arrived, they all went to see Bergetta. As Bergetta slept, Nancy gently touched her hand, and the three siblings, Sally, Bob, and Nancy, gathered around their mother's bed. Bob and Sally felt strongly that Bergetta should be in a hospital. They thought it would be the best for her. On the other hand, Nancy had been trying to fulfill their mother's wishes. Bergetta opened her eyes, looked at her three children and said, "Love one another." Nancy stayed up all night with her mom massaging her feet and stroking her face.

Burggraf family at Bergetta Harris' funeral in 1995. First row: Zach, Nick, Amy Jo, Natalie. Second row: Frank, Char, Nancy, Bernie, Becky, Joan. Third row: Charlie, Heather, Mike, Sally, Mark. Fourth row: Melissa, Megan, Meghan, Annie, Katie, Jenny, Rick.

"Mom is dying," Nancy wrote in her journal. "It is so hard to see her in such pain. She has lost so much weight. Her mind is sharp, and she has her humor but rests a lot. We are caring for her as best we can."

After struggling all day on December 27th, Bergetta slept for hours without moving. When she woke, Bergetta quoted the Bible and the 23rd Psalm over and over until it became hard for her to speak. At 9:13 p.m., she died. Nancy wrote, "She is at peace, pain free—but oh, boy. I'm feeling so sad I can't stand it." Nancy went out into the snow in her mother's front yard and made snow angels. The family wrote the obituary, picked out the casket, and planned the funeral with Pastor Lou. "It was a very hard, but beautiful funeral," wrote Nancy. "All pews filled, a tribute for a great lady who will be missed. A new year beginning, an era ends." It was heartbreaking for them to dismantle Bergetta's house.

Could the memories and stress of Bergetta's death in 1995 have caused Nancy to lose her speech and need a psychiatrist two years later? The thought haunted her. She knew there had to be other answers.

• • •

In January 1998, Nancy cross-stitched and knitted gifts for people while keeping up her store schedule. She thanked God for her continued energy to skate while she prayed for her "voice miracle." From her deck, Nancy put raisins out for "her robins" and noted the rising and setting of the sun. She experienced anxious, sleepless nights with heart palpitations and throbbing legs. Her journals were sprinkled with UND and Roseau hockey scores with notes scratched in such as, "too much stick work that the refs ignored." She said that her life had become boring, except for God, and that she was searching for the Holy Spirit to lead her. "A robin flew, sat on a branch, and chirped at me. I talked to him," she wrote.

In March of 1998, Nancy felt that God had answered one of her prayers. A neurologist had said her paralyzed voice had not been caused by a stroke. "Good news," she wrote. Also in March, Bernie and Nancy traveled to Orlando for two weeks to spend some time in the

sun. While there, she ended up in the hospital because of difficulty swallowing. Her diaphragm was affected, and the couple returned home where Nancy had an MRI and X-rays of the spine and vocal chords. She wrote, "It's good news, it's not the diaphragm."

Following the trip to Orlando, Nancy wrote in her journal after visiting her parents' gravesite. (Her father had died in 1973.) "What my mother taught me, how to be clean, how to be nice, neat and not careless. I miss my mom and dad. What my father taught me, to do everything right! My father was strict and a good friend."

In May, Nancy went to another neurologist in Grand Forks. She was given Prozac after this visit, and the medication made her dizzy. "This new medicine is worse," she wrote. The doctor spoke to her about the possibility of hypnosis and biofeedback. He noticed at this time that her muscles were quivering and twitching. "Hope it's not serious," she wrote. Doctors found no evidence of cancer. "Good news," she wrote. Between doctor's appointments and her "normal" life, Nancy noticed the baby squirrels in her backyard and took apples out to the deer. She did lots of fishing and praying that she could talk again some day. She asked Pastor Lou if he would come soon and place his hands on her for healing. During this time, Nancy wrote that an acquaintance had filled her with guilt when she said, "You have let Satan in—that's what is wrong with your voice." On October 20, 1998, after continued nights when Nancy didn't fall asleep until four or five in the morning, Pastor Lou anointed her with healing oil.

On October 25th, Bernie drove Nancy to her psychiatrist's appointment in Grand Forks. A couple from Roseau were also in the waiting room to see a neurologist.

Bernie shared their story with them. "At first we thought Nancy had a stroke, so we checked that out for six months. Then we thought she had a tumor so we trucked around and checked that out for six months. Then we thought it was depression because we thought her mother's death had caused this. So we're visiting the psychiatrist."

Around the corner the neurologist happened to hear the Burggraf name. He came into the waiting room. "My wife told me she saw you in the mall," he said to Nancy. "She said she was shocked about your slurred speech."

"Stick out your tongue." He took a look and motioned to Nancy. "Come with me."

The physician took Nancy into the exam room where she began to move and shake. "You could see her," Bernie recalled, "moving about like a horse would try to shake off a fly."

The doctor called in another neurologist and his nurse.

"Be in Fargo at 10 a.m. tomorrow," he told the Burggrafs. "We need a second opinion." In Fargo, they met Dr. Garness and had more tests run.

On October 26, 1998, Nancy wrote. "Dr. Garness is a very special lady. She said I have ALS, Lou Gehrig's disease. I had an EMG. Deteriorating muscles."

"And that's when we found out she had rapid onset ALS," said Bernie. "The doctor was very candid and up front. There was no cure but there was hope, and Nancy was in excellent physical condition."

The doctor explained to the Burggrafs that the disease, most often associated with 1939 Yankees' first baseman, Lou Gehrig, affected either the limbs or the speech. In Nancy's case, it was the speech that was affected first. ALS (Amyotrophic Lateral Sclerosis) is a progressive degeneration of the nerve cells in the brain and spinal cord that control the voluntary muscles. One in five people live longer than five years, but death generally occurs within two to ten years after diagnosis. In time, muscles stop receiving messages from the brain and begin to waste away.

"Devastating," Nancy wrote.

A Battle We Were Guaranteed to Lose

⟡⟡⟡

"I didn't get an answer to my prayer,
that everything would be all right,
and I could have my wonderful life back."
—Nancy Burggraf's journal, 1998

March 6, 1999

Game 3, Finals: Roseau Rams vs. Hastings Raiders
The Minnesota State High School Class AA Hockey Championship

At 8:15 p.m. the Roseau Rams, enrollment 339, played the Hastings Raiders, enrollment 1,370. Nearly 16,000 people crowded the Target Center. There was no mistaking the Roseau parents and fans covered in green with their faces painted half white and half green. Their mascot, the Roseau Ram, skated around and led cheers. Roseau fans buzzed about a Hasting's feature story in the hockey program booklet. They felt the media had already awarded the title to Hastings.

Coach Bruce knew that Hastings would come out rockin'. He hoped the Rams could weather that and just keep going. "They will come at us with speed," he said, planning to keep his fourth line fresh and rotate his three lines regularly. "Our game will be won in our end. We have to be a team."

Bernie turned on the television and raised the hospital bed so Nancy could see the game.

October 1998

The night her mother came home after the ALS diagnosis, Cook sat while Nancy took her bath, a nightly ritual. Nancy was angry and she pounded on her legs and shook her head, upset that her body wasn't working. Cook told her right then that she was committed to her mother's needs.

Cook had also been reading about ALS and learned that eventually it paralyzes the muscles needed to breathe. Sometimes people with ALS develop pneumonia because they can't swallow, and they inhale oral secretions into their lungs. Cook realized, however, that the disease would leave her mom's intellect intact and would spare her senses of sight, hearing, smell, taste, and touch. That knowledge gave her some comfort.

In the days following the confirmation of ALS, word began to filter through the hockey world. The idea to nominate Nancy for the United States Hockey Hall of Fame began to pop into hockey conversations. She would be the first woman ever nominated. Rough men who played a tough game sent well wishes. "I got a lump in my throat when people called," recalled Bernie. "They knew her and they loved her."

Some players who lived far from Roseau said they hoped that someone was there to lift her spirits. Others expressed how sad they were and how valuable she had been to the hockey world. It was not only affecting people in Roseau but people all over Minnesota and the United States. A few did not realize the seriousness of the illness and thought that Nancy would pull through. Aaron Broten was surprised because Nancy had always been so vital. "It's tough to deal with," he said. "But it is the reality that we are human and people get sick and die. She was a woman of great faith."

Burggraf trainer Mike Carlson thought that finally naming her disease helped Nancy have some peace of mind. "On one hand it was very sad, but on the other it was a relief for Nancy and the family to figure out what was wrong with her. Nancy always remained nice and calm when she couldn't speak, never got upset."

• • •

Nancy attempted to talk in a slurred, hoarse voice but breathing became more difficult. Bernie remained determined to fight. Even the doctor had told them, "Maybe you can beat this." After studying new ALS research, Frank told Nancy, "Now we drop the gloves and go at it.

We're going to fight it." He looked into amino acid studies, and encouraged his mother to stay active, take antioxidant supplements, vitamin E, and creatine. Nancy, however, was apprehensive about Frank's ideas because she knew she had the worst type of rapid onset ALS, which affected the voice first.

The disease, which is hard to diagnose, is rarer in women and about 20,000 Americans are afflicted with it. Some cases are inherited but most, like Nancy's, occur randomly with no associated risk factors.

Nancy approached her disease deliberately, thoughtfully, professionally. She read, researched, and told Bernie about exercise plans, diets, and positive attitudes. She hoped to turn a sharp decline in muscle control into a long, gentle slide. And yet, she pointed skyward and scribbled on her pad, "God has a plan, and His is the best." Her game face slipped occasionally as she listened to Bernie recall names of past players who were sending her notes and forwarding letters to the Hockey Hall of Fame nominating committee. Some had been uncertain players who had grown into stars because of her. She wrote on her pad to Bernie, "I want my precious life back." Sometimes her thoughts lingered on dying, but she tried not to let this get out of hand. "I want to live each day and appreciate it," she wrote from her living room couch in her notebook. "It's easy to communicate with Bernie. Forty-three years of marriage will do this." Mentally, she decided to live each day with energy, humor, and grace, no differently than how she lived her whole life. Bernie watched her wage this battle. "She was a true champion," he said.

Her prayer partner Eleanor thought Nancy was angry at her illness but not at God. "She reached acceptance," said Eleanor. "She said, 'If this is what I have to face, I will face it.' She was my friend in the Lord. We always talked like we had never been apart, and we still prayed for her health in the basement of the store."

Skating assistant, Diann, saw the ALS come on gradually while she and Nancy worked with the kids on Saturdays. "As it progressed," said Diann, "she never really said anything about it. It wasn't something she mentioned, but it ended up affecting the whole community, everybody, not just hockey. It was hard to see, and we were together to the bitter end."

Coming home for Christmas break to work at the store, Jeremy was surprised at Nancy's failing speech. Her conversations with him were still encouraging and her insights were profound and packed into one or two sentences written to him on pieces of paper. Now he wished he would have kept those writings. "I prayed," he remembers, as Nancy nodded her head in agreement. "She'd give me that same old hug and send me off. But I knew that ALS was serious; I knew it was going to take her life. I wished I could remember more of my meetings with her that Christmas. I thought she was fighting the illness, but she knew that when the time came for her to go, she was going to be all right."

Rick regrets that their family was so competitive, even when it came to trying to fight the illness. "I don't know if we allowed Mom to express herself through the disease," he said. "We were working so hard to support her, we didn't let her communicate what she was really feeling. We were trying so hard to beat the disease and ignore the inevitable that we missed out on an opportunity. You could see it in her eyes that she was frustrated but not able to communicate it. I guess as competitive people, we were fighting a battle we were guaranteed to lose."

Nancy still went to work at the store and kept up with her housecleaning, laundry, and visiting terminally ill patients at the hospital. Walking the streets of Roseau, Nancy had no voice, but she smiled and waved her hellos. While Frank continued to work with hockey camps and clinics, Nancy still evaluated individual skaters by looking at their tapes. Frank would never give up the camps; his mother had taught him to persevere. "I feel bad," Frank remembers because she'd still want to go to the clinics, but she couldn't talk. "She couldn't communicate. And so she'd start writing stuff down. I didn't slow down enough to let her write. It was hard."

A local motel manager offered Nancy regular use of the heated motel pool and changing room. When Bernie offered to pay for services, which they hoped would build up Nancy's lungs, the manager said, "It's payback time for all that Nancy has done."

November and December of 1998, even as Nancy's muscles deteriorated, she and Bernie went to the ice arena. Local children

Image © Star & Tribune/Minneapolis-St. Paul 2009

Having lost the ability to speak, Nancy Burggraf communicates with her husband, Bernie, during their morning coffee at the cafe next to their clothing store in downtown Roseau, Minnesota.

skated toward Nancy wanting attention and hugs. She took time to touch each child while giving them a thumbs-up, sometimes writing notes to them. Bernie carried her bag, laced up her skates for her, and prompted her like a coach. "Skate hard," he yelled at her from the stands as Nancy moved tentatively across the ice. "Close the lanes, and hit 'em when the ref's not looking."

"Hey, rookie," he shouted as Nancy gripped the side boards for balance. "Come on, stride out there."

After 46 years in business, the Burggrafs made a heart-wrenching decision. Because of Nancy's ALS, they decided to sell the store. Bernie said they made the decision together and then told the local newspaper that "there were a lot of good memories, a lot of laughs, and a lot of tricks." On December 26, 1998, a full-page announcement appeared in the Roseau paper: "The Store that was more than a Store" was closing its doors.

Handing over the gavel: Bernie decides against running for mayor in 1998.

Then, another decision. After twelve years of service as the mayor of Roseau and a city council member for eighteen years, Bernie decided to give up the office of mayor to spend more time with Nancy. Often, he would care for her during the night, even carrying her to the bathroom as Nancy got weaker. "She ain't heavy, she's my wife," he said, teasing through the sorrow. Bernie said to the local newspaper that he would still remain active in northwest Minnesota politics, and he told state senators publicly that he would "not be afraid to go to the plate for something, but he would not be a puppet for anybody." He credited Nancy with his ability to be mayor, talking positively, and coaching him. "Do what's right," Nancy had always advised him. "Stand for it. If there's anything that's wrong and you're in doubt, check it out first." Local leaders tried to persuade him to run again, but he decided to leave with regrets. "We've had some great times here," he said in his resignation speech.

Roseau was a small town, but politics could be fierce. Bernie had always tried to make things interesting. Council meetings were at 5:30 p.m. and Bernie's jokes or off-hand remarks would often get a chuckle. And he didn't mind butting heads, such as when Roseau battled Warroad for the location of the county seat. He often took the local newspaper to task about how events were reported. "Shame on you," he'd say, "if you are not a cheerleader for your community."

Some politicians say that Bernie reminded them of George Peppard, the star of the television shows *Banacheck* and *The A-Team*. It must have been his haircut or his semi-cocky manner. He often sent story ideas about local people to the paper. He knew that local business deals were important, but it was people and their achievements that kept the spirit of the community alive.

Another tough decision awaited Nancy. At Bernie's advice, she agreed to sell her red cherry '98 Mustang convertible with white leather seats. She loved that car. Melissa, the oldest grandchild, felt a sense of grief to see that Mustang go. It brought the reality of her grandmother's illness even closer. "When I was fourteen," recalled Melissa, "Nana needed to clean snow off her driveway. She let me take that car and drive up and down the street so she could shovel. She just told me to stay between two points and let me go."

Her other grandchildren remembered how cool their grandmother looked in that Mustang wearing her red Reebok high-top tennis shoes. Nancy wore jeans and sweatshirts and always seemed younger and more fun than anyone else's grandmothers. The grandkids and Nancy also drove to the Roseau Fair each summer singing "John Jacob Jingle Heimer Schmidt" at the top of their lungs. When cruising Main Street Roseau with a granddaughter driving, they blasted the *Lion King* soundtrack, and Nancy ducked down so the girls could wave at cute boys.

Granddaughter Heather remembers when Nancy asked her to drive to hockey camp in Fargo from Grand Forks, where Nancy had been working with the Sioux. "Of course I said yes. Who wouldn't want to drive that car? It was an awesome vehicle, one that turned heads. In the beginning, she told me I could drive however fast I wanted but that it would be my ticket. She asked me if I wanted her to get her fuzz-buster out. She was a riot!"

And so, the red cherry Mustang convertible with white leather seats was gone, a symbol that a woman who loved a little glitz and speed on ice, water, and the road was slowing down.

In January 1999, the University of North Dakota honored Nancy prior to a UND vs. University of Minnesota–Duluth (UMD) game, a fierce interstate rivalry. The Burggraf family assisted a weakened Nancy onto the ice. Engelstad Arena darkened as the spotlight found Nancy, who through the applause raised her thumb. Each Sioux player skated out, greeted her with a single red rose, and hugged her. As the athletic director was about to speak, a lone player emerged in the spotlight, skating from the opposing UMD bench. Jeff Scissions had made the decision to skate out and honor Nancy. She had also trained him in clinics and he remained grateful. He skated out with a single red rose, handed it to Nancy, and gave her a hug. She lifted her thumb. Jeff said later, "I had to do this for Nancy. She did so much for me." The sportscasters were overwhelmed and commented they had never seen anything like this from an opposing team member. "This kid got this idea all on his own," said one announcer.

The athletic director continued. He presented Nancy with a plaque and a bouquet of flowers from UND and read the plaque, "This award is presented to Nancy Burggraf for your years of outstanding support and dedication to the University of North Dakota Fighting Sioux team. Your loyalty, compassion, and expertise has had a direct influence on thousands of hockey players and made them better people. For this, we would like to extend a warm 'Fighting Sioux' thank you." Sioux senior David Hoogsteen presented another bouquet to Nancy and gave her a hug, as did team members Trevor Hammer, Adam Calder, Mike Commodore, and Jason Blake.

A few days later, the community of Roseau honored Nancy at Memorial Arena before a Roseau hockey game. The '99 Rams had lost only one game that season and hockey buffs were predicting a run at the state title. They were her boys, her Rams. Nancy came out on the ice with assistance from Bernie and her five children. The Roseau High School Band began to play, resonating though the big barn arena. After a few musical phrases, the crowd recognized "Wind Beneath My Wings."

As the band played, players skated by Nancy, tipping their hockey sticks to her. She received a bouquet of flowers and each player removed his helmet revealing tears of grief and gratitude. For more than a decade, Nancy had taught them how to take flight on the ice, to find the wind beneath their wings. Now it was time to honor her.

Head coach Bruce and athletic director Terry Gotziaman read a tribute to Nancy for her years of service and presented her with a plaque. Nancy stood demurely with her family, looked small, weak, and uncomfortable with the accolades, but to all players she gave a thumbs-up. She was not comfortable in the spotlight but did not want to disappoint her boys as they stood as an honor guard across the ice.

Inside she knew they had the right stuff to win the state tournament. She made a promise to keep on writing notes to remind them to keep their sticks down and their heads up.

Nancy began to write more and more notes about her illness to her family. "We are all dying," she wrote to Frank, "some of us just at a faster rate."

"I'll admit that I was afraid of death," said Frank. "I was afraid to look at my parent in a casket. I went through it at a younger age with Grandpa and Grandma, and it was something I really feared to have happen this fast. I thought I would struggle more than I did. From a faith standpoint, I know there is something more."

Charlie lived in Minneapolis, six hours away from Nancy during her illness, and it was difficult for him and his family to visit. He saw his mother's diagnosis as a journey everyone will have to take someday. The hard part for him was that his mother wasn't done living. "She had been so active and was trapped," Charlie said. "It made her question God and pray for a miracle." She wrote Charlie a note

Image © Star & Tribune/Minneapolis-St. Paul 2009

Nancy Burggraf, 68, never played a game of hockey, but that didn't stop her from teaching hockey players how to skate for many years.

When Nancy Burggraf showed up at the ice arena in Roseau, she drew a crowd of youngsters. She taught hockey players how to skate faster and more effectively since 1971. The boys who tried her techniques found they could skate through other players and leave them twisted like pretzels.

Image © Star & Tribune/Minneapolis-St. Paul 2009

that said, "I don't think I'm going to get my miracle." Charlie felt so helpless because he and his mother connected spiritually, and he didn't have an answer. "I didn't know what to say or do. It's just the nature of being on this planet. But it was hard to see her die slowly. She lived trying not to be a burden to other people. But my sisters really served her, and Cook in particular because she was the one who lived right there in Roseau."

Charlie couldn't escape the guilt of not being able to be there. "We decided as a family to be as gracious as we could toward one another and not be weird as to who wasn't going to be here because we couldn't control the timetable on Mom's illness," Charlie remembers.

For Becky, it was hard to realize that her mom was failing. She wanted a quick fix, to say, "Just snap out of it, Mom, okay? Get a grip. Take a vitamin or something to get better."

"Just being around my mom in her weak state," said Becky, "just knowing what she had gone through when her mother had died and her frustrations, I tried hard not to repeat those kinds of things where families get torn apart from the stress of the situation."

Nancy stopped writing in her journal on January 31, 1999. Her journal had been her confidant since 1987, and her last words in it read, "I found out I really need the PEG (feeding tube). Sob," followed by a drawing of a frowning face and tears streaming from both eyes. "I also found out my diaphragm doesn't move so my breathing is impaired," she continued. "The surgeon recommended the PEG, but I'm concerned because it may shut down my breathing. Today I couldn't breathe. I spent the whole day vegging out on the couch. I wasted the whole day. God forgive me. Watched the Sioux win again. Really pooped. Watched *Touched by an Angel* on TV. Day ends. Sob."

Nancy knew when she walked out the door of her house to enter Roseau Regional Hospital that she would never return. The clock was counting down for her. She had dropped to 93 pounds and was unable to feed herself. The ALS that silenced her vocal muscles had destroyed her ability to swallow. She had written over and over again in her journal, "I'm having a bad day; I can't breathe; I can't eat. Sob." And once again the down-turned smile with tears. The feeding tube became a symbol of giving up for her, and she was fearful of the surgery to insert the tube. A few years earlier, she had experienced a difficult time with anesthesia during a routine gall bladder surgery. She didn't like losing control and being "put under." All the while, Nancy tried to put on the Burggraf game face like she had taught so many hockey players to do. How could she give up and admit defeat? Because of the feeding tube, she would be dependent and weak.

Where is God in all this? she wondered. Had she not been a faithful servant? Had she not read and memorized her Bible? Hadn't she prayed at length for others who were ill? Had she not lived the Gospel telling others about her faith? Nancy lamented just as Job had done in the Old Testament when he said, "I know there must be someone in heaven who will come at last to my defense. Even after my skin is eaten by disease, while still in this body, I will see God. I will see him with my own eyes, and he will not be a stranger," Job 19:25–27.

Nancy entered the hospital on February 1, 1999 after having watched what she called a "boring" Super Bowl game. She continued to have a pad of paper in the hospital bed with her, and she communicated with notes to hospital staff, family, and friends. She wrote this final letter to her family:

Dear Children:

This part of my life is devastating. I am trying my hardest to hang on to my faith that God really loves me and will help me. His timing is perfect, but my frustration is mounting.

I, deep inside me, feel the real problem came too late. I read in an ALS book than when ALS attacks the breathing and speech, those people don't live long. It is hard to take medicine when it makes me feel worse.

I have been scheduled for an upper GI endoscopy—it's where they put a tube into the stomach to nourish the body. I don't want to do this. It is just another thing to frustrate me.

My swallowing is getting worse. My energy level is so low I can't do anything.

All the baskets full of prayers are, so far, of no avail. I will keep the faith, trusting that God will eventually do something.

I'm not afraid to die. This body is so disgusting. It will be hard to leave family, but God will allow me to watch on high.

Love you,
M

In the following days, a parade of well wishers, community members, hockey players, and neighbors visited Nancy's room. Some came to massage her feet and hands because Nancy had done this for them or for their relatives; Eleanor and Pastor Lou came to pray with

her. "She was very insistent," said Lou, "that I would do her funeral service. She pointed at me, then at her, then folded her hands on her chest. I'd assure her that nothing would change; I would do her funeral."

Skating partner Diann came by to report on the Saturday skating sessions she had taken over from Nancy, and she also talked about hunting, snowmobiling, and killing a deer (she had also cried after the successful hunt). For many years, Diann had cut Nancy's hair and they shared the same style: short, no frills, a "no hair" look as they described it. "I cut her hair in the hospital," recalled Diane, "for the last time."

Becky, Rick, and Frank came as they could from Fargo; Charlie and brother Bob from Minneapolis; Sally from Arizona; and Bernie, Cook, and Cook's daughters Megs and Natalie visited Nancy every day. Nancy busied herself playing tic-tac-toe, promising to beat anyone who challenged her. Members of the Emergency Medical squad stopped in between ambulance runs. They were surprised to see that Nancy had organized all her EMT training books, and she gave them away to each of the squad members. Cook and Becky, both dental hygienists and trained in medical procedures, helped out the nursing staff in the late evenings by suctioning their mother's lungs so it was easier for her to breathe. They, like Nancy did for Bergetta four years before, were not afraid to touch, bathe, caress, and hold their dying mother.

Nancy started off in a regular hospital room but was eventually moved to a hospice care room within the hospital, room 205. This particular room was set up for a hospice caregiver or a family member to be there around the clock. As Nancy worked through her illness with dignity, Bernie continued to coach. "People have to move on," he said. "You can't just throw in the towel and ride into the sunset. You have to fight through it."

14

The Rams Roar

"I have to get a shut-out for her. I promised her."
—*Jake Brandt, goalie on 1999 Roseau Ram team*

March 6, 1999—8:15 p.m.

Finals Continue:
The Minnesota State High School Class AA Hockey Championship

The sports reporter began:

At 5'7", Junior Jake "The Snake" Brandt stands tall in the goal for the title game. The Raiders come out rockin' and pepper Jake like it's a turkey shoot. Hastings wants to roll the dice, go for a "quick kill," and get a lead on the Rams they couldn't overcome. But someone forgot to tell Jake Brandt. Jake is an all-state goalie who takes a dim view of the goal judge turning on the red light behind his net. Jake stops 11 big shots in the first period, and the Raiders are asking themselves, "Whatcha gotta do to score on this kid?" Good thing the Raiders come up with goose eggs because the Rams are back on their heels, off balance, out of system. After 13 minutes of the Raiders attack, the Rams settle down and go to work. The Rams are back in their game. This means trouble for the Raiders.

In the second period, "Big O" breaks the scoreless tie and puts the puck over the left shoulder of the goalie. Twenty-three seconds later at 7:03, David Klema drills the puck off a Raider's facemask and the Rams lead 2-0. In the third period, the Rams put the

Raiders in a deeper hole. Mike Klema scores with three seconds remaining in the power play. And the Rams aren't done yet. At the 5:24 Mark, Matt Erickson registers his second goal of the tourney. At 4-0 the Rams capture their sixth state title.

"All I was thinking during the first period was I have to stop the shots for her," said Jake Brandt. "I have to get a shut-out for Nancy. I promised her."

As the last seconds of the game ticked off, Phil Larson broke down on the bench from all the emotion. "At the end of the first period, I knew we had to settle down and play," he said. "I looked at the other players and we all knew we had to play our game. When we got our first goal, you could feel it in our hearts."

"I was under Nancy's hospital bed for the first thirteen minutes," said Bernie. "But then you could see it start. The Rams went to work.

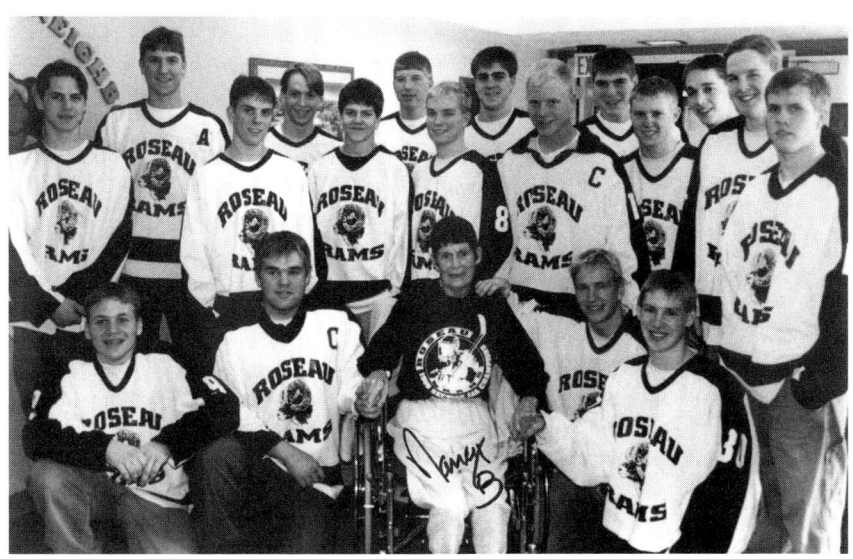

The 1999 Roseau Rams with Nancy Burggraf at Roseau Memorial Hospital. Front row, left to right: Aaron Degerness, Paul Baumgartner, Nancy, Mike Klema, Jake Brandt. Middle row: Tony Erickson, Luke Erickson, Ryan Fevold, Matt Erickson, Phil Larson, Jesse Modahl, Derrick Byfuglien, Parry Eidsmoe. Back row: Josh Olson, David Klema, Bobby John Byfuglien, Mark Fabain, Erik Fabian, Ross Miller.

They played the body, moved the puck, total teamwork, total mastery of this great game."

But the excitement wasn't over yet. Four Rams made the all-state team; Bruce got Coach of the Year, his assistant was honored as Assistant Coach of the Year, the school received the Sportsmanship Award, the cheerleaders the Spirit Award, and the team an academic all-state title. At the medal ceremony, the Rams players, one after the other, turned to the cameras, held up their medals, and shouted, "For you, Nancy." When the cameras recorded the entire Rams team, they piled up and danced in celebration. They shouted in unison as they held their trophy high overhead, "One, two, three, Nancy, we love you. This is for you." Even the broadcasters, who had been mentioning the dedication to Nancy Burggraf throughout the tournament, didn't know what to do with this one, as their voices broke with emotion.

From her hospital bed, Nancy tried to respond to what she had just heard. She shook her legs; she pounded her hands lightly next to her body. Her eyes widened and she tried to speak. She listened as the newscaster interviewed Phil Larson.

"She has been with us since we were seven or eight years old," he said. "We didn't even like the drills she did with us at that age. We didn't realize what she was doing for us. She has been our secret weapon."

"Oh, brother," said Bernie after the game. "We both felt appreciated, teary-eyed, lump in the throat, all of the above. It reflects the character of this team, their heart, concern, humanity, class. It reflects on their parents who held high standards for them. It reflects on all who have coached and tutored them. They have showcased what Roseau is all about, having your head on straight, being focused, and again, having class."

Cook, in the room with Nancy and Bernie, said of the moment, "We had no idea the team was going to do this. This was my mother's affirmation, on her deathbed, that what she had been doing all these years was good."

Bernie and Nancy received phone calls from across the Midwest, from friends, legislators, and strangers who were so moved by the actions of this group of young men. At the time of their greatest victory, these players took the time to remember someone who meant

1999 Championship Hockey Team. Back row, left to right: Coach Bruce Olson, Assistant Coach Jim Lundbohm, Ryan Fevold, Parry Eidsmoe, Aaron Degeneress, Luke Erickson. Middle row: Manager Frank Wookey, Anthony (Tony) Erickson, David Klema, Josh Grahn, Bobby John Byfuglien, Erick Fabien, Ross Miller, Nathan Berry, Jacob (Jake) Brandt. Front row: Mark Fabien, Mike Klema, Derrick Byfuglien, Paul Baumgartner, Josh Olson, Phil Larson, Jessie Modahl, Matthew Erickson.

everything to them. Again, calls continued suggesting that Nancy be nominated for the Hall of Fame.

With the blue ribbon around his neck, Phil Larson knew that hard work and teamwork had won the game. The Target Center maintenance crew, who had to do a quick turnaround of the facility, walked onto the ice and asked Phil to leave so they could cover the floor for a concert. Phil nodded, but he didn't want to leave the memory of that place. He skated slowly to the exit.

After the game, Nancy raised her thumb. Closed her eyes. Exhausted.

15

Welcome Home

❧❦❧

March 1999

The Rams had made the trip from the grain silos of Roseau to the skyscrapers of Minneapolis, and their message, "Nancy, we love you. This is for you," had traveled across 400 miles of lakes, forests, rivers, and fields to a room in Roseau Area Hospital where Nancy watched her favorite hockey team one last time.

At the welcome home celebration, 2,000 fans waited at Roseau High School for the team to arrive. But the Rams' first stop was the hospital. The players crowded around Nancy and shared hugs and tears. Cook and hospital staff dressed Nancy and got her up in a chair, so the team could take a picture with her and the trophy. When they left, they placed the trophy on her windowsill until the official ceremony the following evening.

In the gym on Monday, the crowd buzzed. Four of the dads who played in the 1978 Championship Game had sons on the 1999 team. In 1978, Roseau had come in second. One parent said, "I didn't change my lucky sweatshirt all week, stains or no stains." Another said she had been a basket case all week. One dad wore a suit jacket to the game. He said the last time he dressed up was 1990, the last time the Rams won.

"I was completely nervous," said another dad, who said that he had carried it around with him for twenty years that they hadn't won

in 1978. Three players from the '78 team had gone on to the National Hockey League. In that '78 game, Neal Broten hit the post three different times while trying to score.

The official ceremony celebrated Roseau as the "Little Town, Big Champs" with words like "they are all legends now" filtering through the gym. A swarm of kids sought autographs from their new heroes. With a 27-1 record, the championship was an exclamation mark on a terrific season. And goalie Jake Brandt kept smiling through it all.

Mayor Jeff Pellowski used terms like power, dominance, and determination to describe the boys. And above all, the word "class." The mayor and city council proclaimed March 8-12 as Roseau Ram Hockey Team Week. Board of Education member Teresa McDonnell told a story from the Minnesota School Board Association meeting the same week the Rams skated to victory. She was assigned a seat across from the chair of the rival Hastings School District. The Hastings chair introduced himself as chair of the school that was going to win the State AA championships. Teresa bit her tongue, but then when the conference reconvened on Sunday, she asked if she could reintroduce herself.

Another speaker urged players to thank their parents. Coach Bruce thanked the statisticians, the student managers, and the band for providing the "electricity." He gave each player a watch "to make sure they get to school on time." When he presented a watch to the still smiling Jake Brandt, the crowd stood for a standing ovation. The coach shared the feelings that pulsed through the locker room at tourney time. Each senior had spoken to fire up the team. Paul Baumgartner had reminded them all, "Remember, Nancy's watching." The coach concluded, "I feel fortunate to be a small part of this great team."

As master of ceremonies of the celebration, Bernie read letters from state officials, business leaders, and UND coach Dean Blais. Bernie also joked that junior Jake Brandt wouldn't be returning to the team next year because he had been hired as a poster boy for Colgate toothpaste. Athletic director Terry Gotziaman continued with an emotional speech, "Athletics bring a lot of pride to a community. These guys represented the community with the highest regard. Nancy

Burggraf has been an inspiration to the hockey players for many years. Nancy, we love you." These words echoed the crowd's sentiments. Two thousand people gave Nancy a standing ovation.

From the radio in her hospital room, Nancy listened as the applause continued.

For six straight minutes.

Not So Lonely

March 1999

In the three weeks before Easter, Cook's daughter, 16-year-old Megs, spent every free moment she could at the hospital. She would go to school for first period and then go and see her grandmother.

"She opened her eyes," Megs said, "and I could tell she was overwhelmed to see me. I could tell she wanted to talk to me, and it hurt her so badly that she couldn't tell me how she was feeling. She was getting so weak it was hard to read the writing on her notepad."

Megs remembered one day when her grandpa Bernie (she called him "Bumpie") came into the room laughing. "He had just scared the nurses with his rubber snake," Megs said, smiling. "He was such a joker with the nurses. But it was good for us because he always kept a positive attitude. Bumpie loved Nana with all his heart. But he knew she was in so much pain. He wanted her to be happy."

"Hey, hey, Megs. Skippin' school again?" Bernie joked.

"Yep. I wanted to see what Nana was up to."

Megs looked at Nancy and saw the slightest flash of a smile and sparkling eyes. She squeezed Meg's hand, and Megs knew that Nancy was grateful to have her there. Nancy motioned Bernie to come to her. "What's up, babe?"

Nancy pointed to her third finger and one of her diamond rings.

Megs thought Nancy was in pain, so she began to massage her

hands. Then Nancy pointed to Megs and pointed at the ring Bernie had given her. It was Meg's favorite, a square setting with tiny delicate diamond stones. Then she pointed to Megs.

"She wants you to have it," Bernie said.

"I don't think so, Bump. She loves that ring."

Megs looked over to Nancy and saw her grandmother nodding. Megs couldn't believe it. She felt so honored. Tears started when she began to think what it would be like when Nancy was gone. Megs flashed back to the good times—like cruising down Main Street in the Mustang convertible or going for her first snowmobile ride with Nancy, speeding around a curve, and even rolling over once or twice on the snowmobile and coming up laughing uncontrollably. At Nancy's bedside for a few more hours, Megs massaged her feet, rubbed her temples, and read Bible verses to her. She thought it made Nancy relaxed and comfortable. "I never got sick of it," Megs said. "I never wished I was hanging out with my friends instead."

• • •

Home for spring break from college, Jeremy missed his discussions with Nancy in the store basement. He had seen her at Christmas when she was still standing and walking. Now, it struck him that she was dying. She appeared as a worn-out body lying in bed. He noted that the room was dimly lit, not a real sad room, but a comforting blue light gave off shadows in the corners. The light came from a dimmed halogen lamp right over Nancy's bed. Flowers and baskets stood all over the place, and a banner from the Roseau High School hockey team hung near her. It seemed like a hospital room, and yet it seemed like Nancy's room. As he walked in the room holding his guitar case, Jeremy distinctly heard the beeping of the life monitoring equipment. Nancy couldn't greet Jeremy, and he wondered if she understood him when he talked to her. She had always encouraged him, even when ALS had taken her voice. Now, not even her eyes showed recognition.

It was beginning to get dark outside and Jeremy noted the hum of the humidifier and the white tile floor. It was still winter in Roseau,

and the family had draped their coats over pieces of furniture. Eucalyptus leaves stood in a vase and Jeremy remembered Nancy had put them in the store to keep people healthy. When Jeremy's grandmother had been in the nursing home, he brought his guitar to sing for her. It occurred to him that this might be his last time with Nancy, and he thought she might like him to sing for her.

Family members occupied the room across from Nancy's and they came and went, in and out of Nancy's room, and it seemed to Jeremy that they could only handle so much time in the room emotionally. Walking to the side of Nancy's bed, Jeremy held her hand and let her know he was there. He talked about school, what he had been up to, his travels, his life plans. "I'm still in school," he said stroking her hand, "I'm finishing my last semester. I'm going to do my music full-time."

Nancy had predicted this would be his future. She often asked him at the store, "What is God doing in your life?" So, this time he just told her. Then he sat on the edge of her bed, on the left side between her and the window. When only he was in the room, he played whatever came to mind, mostly soothing music, like his version of Psalm 23. When other family members were there, they requested hymns and choruses from church. Nancy stayed asleep. After three days of visiting and playing, Jeremy picked up his guitar and started to put on his coat.

Nancy woke up. She made a small gesture to him with her right hand for him to come close to her. He moved to hold her hand, and she put both hands over her chest. It seemed to him she made praying hands, but her hands were cupped and they didn't quite fit together.

"Do you want me to pray with you?" he asked.

She moved her thumb slightly.

Family members entered and they all prayed together. Jeremy felt Nancy give his hand a small squeeze.

"It was crazy," he later reflected. "This woman I knew to be so full of life, vitality, and passion. Now she seemed smaller than ever and nearly lifeless. I'm sure there were times she got on people's nerves, like the rest of us. But she was a saint to me. Virtually, every time we talked, Nancy gave me spiritual insight."

Jeremy decided to write a song about Nancy and how she had maintained her hope.

. . .

Waking Easter morning, Cook wondered if she should go to church as planned or spend the morning with her mom. Easter had been Nancy's favorite holiday, and she had always decorated Easter baskets for each of her children and grandchildren. Cook's plan was to have the two Burggraf families, who were in town for the holidays, over for Sunday dinner after church. Then they would all go to the hospital. But Cook wavered. She felt drawn to her mother's hospital room. She decided to go and ended up calling Bernie because an April snowstorm had left Cook unable to get out of her driveway.

"Dad," said Cook, picking up her cell phone. "Can you bring me to the hospital? I'm not going to church today. Megs and Nat can help get dinner ready."

"Sure," said Bernie, who was sounding more drawn and tired as Nancy's illness wore on. "I'm on my way. I'll bring the rest of the family after dinner."

Cook arrived at Nancy's hospital room early enough to give her mom a bath.

"Can I help you wash her hair?" asked Anna, the nurse on duty. The family and staff all knew the neat and tailored Nancy, and they wanted to respect her dignity.

"I feel that's just what we should be doing today," said Cook as she and the nurse began Nancy's sponge bath and changed the bedding.

They held Nancy's head over a small plastic tub and washed her short brown hair. The team worked gently and fast since Nancy tired very easily. Finally she was cleaned and lotioned. "You know my mom loves smelly lotions," said Cook, smiling. "She could drop a hundred bucks just like that at Bath & Body Works."

Finally, they put fresh pajamas on her, noting how listless Nancy was, what little expression was in her eyes. She couldn't move her arms, legs, or head. Cook busied herself cleaning Nancy's room, determined to keep everything tidy every day because it had been her mom's way. Rick and Joan relieved Cook after church so she could go home and eat dinner with the rest of the family.

• • •

"Mom," said Megs, who was helping to clean up after Easter dinner. "Can I go to a movie with Jamie this afternoon? She thinks I should get away from the hospital for a while."

"No," said Cook.

"Please, Mom, I haven't done anything for three weeks."

"What if something happens?"

"I'll just be gone for two hours. Nothing has happened in three weeks; why would it happen now?"

"Okay, but don't regret it. Please."

On the way to the movie, Megs went to tell Nancy goodbye and told her she would be back soon. Nancy squeezed her hand, and Megs kissed her cheek. Nancy's skin was soft and smelled of flowers from all her different lotions.

"I love you, Nana," Megs whispered.

Nancy squeezed her hand.

Megs sat in the movie feeling guilty about not being with Nancy. "What kind of person would leave her grandma on her deathbed to go to a movie?" she thought. "Me, that's who." But she decided she deserved two hours away from it all.

• • •

"Cook, you need to come now," said Rick from the hospital phone later that Easter Day. "The nurse is telling us we need to be here, and we shouldn't plan to leave tonight."

In the hospital room, Becky carried on the Easter basket tradition for the family. She gave her mom a basket with a goose Beanie Baby because Nancy always put fake geese on the lawn at Christmas time. For Bernie, she made a duck basket because of his love for Ducks Unlimited and filled it with his favorite jellybeans. It was a sign for Becky when Nancy didn't respond at all to her basket. Becky and her husband Mark were nervous about driving in a snowstorm back to Fargo, but the nurse said, "Everything in Nancy's body is slowing down. Her vital signs are worsening."

An unresponsive Nancy wore a white gown with flowers on the pockets. The granddaughters took turn massaging Nancy's feet, and Becky's daughter, Megan, had painted Nancy's toes red with pink decal hearts. Family members gathered around.

At 5:10 p.m. Nancy's nurse, Anna, monitored respiration levels. The level: 27. Blood pressure: 89/110.

Rick's daughter, Annie, sat by her grandmother and also watched changes in breathing as she jotted the machine readings on a piece of paper.

By 6 p.m. Annie recorded respiration as 22. Blood pressure: 92/76.

As the respiration levels dropped, family members came in and out of the room.

At 6:30 p.m. respiration was 19. Blood pressure: 96/74.

Rick called Pastor Lou and he came right away.

At 7 p.m. respiration was 17. Blood pressure: 88/67.

Becky checked Nancy's pulse. It was so faint she could hardly feel it. The nurse put on the stethoscope and told the family, "Your Mom's spirit is leaving."

Everyone stood or sat around the bed.

"Our father, who art in heaven," Lou began. "Hallowed be thy name," the family joined in.

"I should leave," nurse Anna whispered to Becky.

"No, stay," said Becky. "You have meant so much to my mom. She loved all those foot rubs you gave her. Please stay." And she put her arm around the nurse.

"Thy Kingdom come; thy will be done; on earth as it is in heaven."

Her breathing is so shallow, thought Cook. *If she could only open her eyes and actually say goodbye to us. We haven't heard her voice for nearly two years.*

"Give us this day our daily bread and forgive us our trespasses as we forgive those who trespass against us."

The family placed their hands on Nancy.

"And lead us not into temptation, but deliver us from evil."

Megan, still rubbing Nancy's feet, noticed that they were beginning to turn blue. Natalie, sitting to the left on Nancy's bed, stroked her grandmother's mottled hand.

At 7:30 p.m., Annie reported no respiration, no blood pressure, no pulse.

They heard the final breath. Nancy was at peace.

"For thine is the Kingdom and the power and the glory forever and ever. Amen."

Becky, who knew that the last thing to shut down was the brain, bent over and whispered in her mother's ear, "Mom, I love you. And I'll see you later."

"Mom," said Natalie tugging on Cook's arm, "when I was holding Nana's hand, I felt her squeeze my hand, just a tiny squeeze, right before she died."

Cook and Becky ran outside, without coats, and made snow angels in front of the hospital, exactly what Nancy had done moments after Bergetta's death. The family stayed at Nancy's bedside and continued to touch and talk to their mother. Bernie, who had been trying to keep his game face, left the room to be alone. When he came back, he told his kids, "I hate Sunday nights. Do you know why I hate Sunday nights?" The family was puzzled. "When I was little and my dad died, my mom took a job as a teacher out of town. On Sunday nights she would leave me and not come home til' Friday night. I stayed with my grandma, but I never have liked Sunday nights." And now, Nancy had also left him on a Sunday night.

• • •

"Hey, Megs," said Jamie, after the movie. "Want to go to the store quick before I bring you back to the hospital?"

"Um, yeah, I guess, but it's gotta be really quick," Megs replied. Megs could tell Jamie was getting frustrated and didn't understand what it was like to be losing a loved one. No one understood what it was like for Megs to lose her Nana.

At that moment, Megs needed to talk to her mom.

"Hello, Roseau Area Hospital," answered the nurse.

"Room 205 please," Megs said.

"One sec Megs. It might take a minute for them to answer, okay?" Megs thought the nurse sounded worried.

Why would it take so long to answer? wondered Megs. Maybe they were helping Nancy to the bathroom or something.

"Hello."

"Mom, I'll be right there. The movie just got done and we stopped at…"

"Megs, she's gone," Cook said.

Megs dropped the phone and her body numbed.

Walking through the hospital halls not knowing what to expect, Megs hoped the phone call was a bad dream. She stepped into the room and saw her grandmother. She could still smell Nancy's soaps and lotions. She touched Nancy's hand. Hearing someone behind her, Megs turned and saw Bernie in the doorway. Tears came as she rushed to give him a hug.

"I never got to say goodbye."

"You don't need to say goodbye, Megs, 'cause she's with you all the time now."

Megs took one last look at Nancy, kissed her on the cheek, and went to find her mom. Megs believed in her heart that Nancy was in heaven being rewarded for the many great things she had done for people. She was happy for her Nana.

• • •

Late in the day, Jeremy finished eating an Easter meal with his parents. He began the drive back to school at the University of Minnesota-Morris. It was a beautiful afternoon. Notes, lyrics, and tunes churned in his head as he tried to write a song about Nancy. He couldn't get his thoughts together and was frustrated as he thought about Nancy, her healing ministry, and the fact that she was now dying. A thought popped into his head. One day, Jeremy had told a friend, "I may be alone, but I'm not so lonely." Then he began to sing those lyrics from Nancy's perspective. It wrote itself. Momentarily, in the evening hours, he pulled off the road singing, shaking, crying. He was eager to finish the song. "Later I found out that it was exactly the time that Nancy left this world behind and passed on to heaven," he said. "Not so Lonely" became "Nancy's Song."

Like a Leaf

The funeral home staff waited until everyone had a chance to say goodbye to Nancy in the hospital room. The nursing staff backed away and let the family be with their mother. Megan and her cousin Megs did one last snuggle with their grandma. Frank had brought family home movies to show in the family room and memories of Nancy's life rolled past the family. Nancy, in her blue and white wide pin-striped pants surrounded by five little kids dancing around the Christmas tree. Nancy, riding in the speedboat at Rocky Point cabin. Nancy, skating in the ice revue. Nancy, showing off her golf swing. Nancy, outdoors in her hunting gear. Nancy, giving a birthday present, a new pair of skates.

The nurse offered to pack up Nancy's things, while the family discussed the funeral. They decided it would be a celebration of her life.

Roger Helgeson, the funeral director, stopped by the hospital to visit with the family.

"Roger," said Cook, "I have a box of Mom's hair color left. I promised her I'd color her hair. Okay?"

"Fine by me," he said. "I'll let you know when."

The family went over to Cook's house, sat in the dining room, and plugged in the Christmas tree, which was still up from December. Bathed in the white lights and shadows of the tree, they told stories about their mom. As word of Nancy's death filtered through Roseau and across Minnesota, the Burggraf phone started ringing.

"She exited this world as caring and gently as she treated it," Bernie said to callers. "She drifted off like an autumn leaf floating down from a tree," he said to some. "It was very peaceful. She just floated away with class and dignity."

• • •

On Tuesday, Cook and Becky sat in the waiting room of the funeral home ready to color Nancy's hair.

They entered the preparation room.

"She's so beautiful," Cook whispered. "She looks so peaceful. Her skin is beautiful."

Becky found a CD player at the funeral home and by coincidence a Neil Diamond CD, the very one Nancy used for hockey warm-ups. With "Cracklin' Rosie" playing in the background, the women began the final act of love for their mother, coloring and styling her hair "Nancy-style."

There is peace in this room, thought Cook, as she found strength to do this last ministry. She accepted that Nancy was no longer suffering, and she was grateful she had shared in taking care of Nancy throughout her illness. Cook caught a glimpse of Nancy's toes.

"Her feet look good," said Cook, smiling, as she saw the little hearts painted on Nancy's toenails.

The daughters picked out Nancy's prettiest dress and shoes for the funeral, sprayed on her signature cologne, and then sprinkled glitter on her and the floor around the casket, which was made from oak, Nancy's favorite wood.

In the funeral home chapel, the family placed two hospital IV stands to flank Nancy's casket. Her ice skates hung from them along with the disco ball, and her fringed, rhinestoned, and glittered skating uniforms. With Neil Diamond crooning "Cracklin' Rosie" in the background, Becky and Cook posed in skating positions while Roger snapped one last picture of them with their mother.

Borning Cry

Friday, April 9, 1999

More than 500 people crowded into Messiah Lutheran Church. A damp spring wind blew down Highway 11 and across the Roseau landscape, and clouds covered the sun. A fitting day for a funeral, people mentioned as they walked into the Messiah sanctuary. Spring was trying to happen at the tip of northern Minnesota, but it didn't come easily. It took a while to shake off winter for good. Occasionally the sun broke through the clouds, sending a beam to illuminate the stained-glass windows.

Those who couldn't find seating in the pews or extra chairs in the aisles lined the walls and doorways for the celebration of Nancy's life. "Keep your game faces," Bernie encouraged the family. The EMT squad entered the church in full uniform, passed and nodded in front of Nancy's casket and filled the last pew. It was a fitting spot for them to sit, since the EMT's job required them to be vigilant, on the lookout for emergencies in large crowds. Along with IV stands, the disco ball, skating uniforms, and skates, 97 baskets of flowers nearly overwhelmed the front of the sanctuary with their color explosion, a drastic contrast to the bitter cold whiteness outside.

The UND charter bus pulled into the parking lot, and Coach Dean Blais and 30 members of the Sioux hockey team, dressed in their Sioux blazers, entered the Messiah doors. They were the honorary pallbearers along with the 30 members of the Roseau State High School Championship Team. Led by captains Phil Larson, Paul Baumgartner, and Josh Olson, the Rams, wearing their green and white jerseys, followed behind the casket and the family and grandchildren, who were the official pallbearers.

Pastor Lou, Nancy's confessor and confidant, had been given the word that the family didn't want much said about her suffering. So, the opening hymn was a real rouser, the 23rd Psalm sung to the tune of the "Happy Wanderer."

"The Lord's My Shepherd, I'll not want. He makes me down to lie. In pastures green, he leadeth me, the quiet waters by."

The congregation boomed out the words to the song, announcing the grand celebration. The Helgeson brothers ushered Nancy's casket, slowly down the center aisle followed by family, grandchildren, UND players, and Roseau Rams. The processional nearly overpowered Lou.

Lou's memories of Nancy began like instant replay in his head as the procession moved toward him. He remembered her laughter. If something went wrong in a church service, Nancy would be sure to needle him afterward. Or if something happened with her or the business, he teased her. He recalled when he anointed her with oil as an affirmation of her healing ministry, and he remembered her seeking and praying about God's will for her life. He recalled in the last days of her life and how she was so insistent that he do her funeral service. That promise was about to be made good. A single note card sat on the pulpit with one sentence written on it. He joked about it, using a standard preacher's line, "I'm letting the spirit move me."

Lou began, "We have gathered to celebrate Nancy's life, Nancy's walk of faith. She touched so many lives. Now she has a new life."

He related the story from the hospital when he and Nancy were visiting. "Nancy turned her eyes toward the window," he said, "and raised her hand. I asked if she wanted the Lord to come for her, and she nodded. After that I prayed God would answer her quickly as she wished."

Sitting in the pew with other Roseau players, Matt Erickson leaned over to Mark Fabian, "Hey, I smell her. I smell Nancy's perfume."

"I know," said Mark. "I keep hearing her whistle in my head. It's like she wants us to change drills."

Then Lou read from Isaiah 55. "My thoughts, says the Lord, are not like yours, and my ways are different from yours. As high as the heavens are above the earth, so high are my ways and thoughts above yours."

And when Job spoke in Chapter 19:23-27. "How I wish that someone would remember my words and record them in a book! Or with a chisel carve my words in stone so they would last forever. But I know there is someone in heaven who will come at last to my defense. Even after my skin is eaten by disease, while still I am in this body I will see God. I will see him with my own eyes, and he will not be a stranger."

Sitting in the pew, Lee Goren from the Sioux remembered Nancy "glowing" as she pretended to pound goals into his hockey stick. He couldn't help but smile, even at a funeral. "She's probably the greatest person I've ever known," he thought.

David Hoogsteen, also of the Sioux, had memories of Nancy putting her heart and soul into Sioux hockey. Once, when he did something good on the ice, Nancy took time to give him a reward, a new cap, he remembered.

"Nancy was a woman of prayer," Lou went on with the service. "I know that. I know it well. Nancy and I prayed in the sanctuary, in my office, in her home, at the store. I know she prayed for me. And she prayed for you."

Stan Kindzerski, Messiah choir member and friend of Nancy's, sang the hymn "Borning Cry," in which one line reads, "If you find someone to share your time and you join your hearts as one, I'll be there to make your verses rhyme from dusk till' rising sun." The hundreds of people remembered Nancy with them at home, at the arena, in the store, in the outdoors. It might have been an attitude check or maybe a time of quiet prayer. Nancy made their verses rhyme with her encouraging words. These words touched UND coach Dean Blais, who felt like Nancy was a part of his family and his players' families. Dean had said that Nancy's death was devastating to him and to the hockey world.

Rick spoke for the family. "Thank you to all of you. We will remember you forever. Thank you to the Roseau Hockey Team for winning the state championship for our mother. Thank you to the Sioux. Thank you to our dad for being an incredible example of living your marriage vows. I never knew how hard it was for people to go through this kind of loss. But all of you coming to say you are sorry will help us through."

Lou and Bernie had sifted through the letters that had been sent in honor of Nancy. Bernie was insistent that Lou read them so people would get a "feeling" for what was said in the letters. One letter said, "You taught me what it means to be a character player, on and off the ice. You had a lot to do with making me the hockey player I am today. I will hold you close to my heart forever." Another read, "You may never have scored a goal, but you made a record number of assists. Your memory will live for years to come. U.S. hockey is very fortunate to have been loved and positively influenced by you." And another, "I have not lived very long, twenty-five years, but throughout my travels, there is no one with more class than Nancy Burggraf."

Then Pastor Lou offered this poem:

When I come to the end of the road, the sun has set for me.
I want no rites as a gloom filled room. Why cry for a soul set free?
Miss me a little but not too long, and now with your head bowed low.
Remember the love that we once shared. Miss me, but let me go.

At the close of the service, Larry Pladson played a tribute to Nancy, the Lord's Prayer on his saxophone, and then the congregation sang Nancy's favorite hymn, "Joy to the World."

The UND Sioux bus and the Rams bus led the funeral procession out the parking lot and onto Main Street. The family requested that only players and family members come to the burial site. The procession slowed as they allowed Nancy one last pass in front of the arena. The mourners continued south on Highway 11, about three miles west of the city limits, before turning left across the railroad tracks and into Moe/Rose Lutheran Cemetery.

"You'll appreciate this place we picked," Bernie had told Lou. He and Nancy found it together. "It's even on a little hill so the view looking south is fabulous."

Specially handcrafted wren houses hung in the trees surrounding Nancy's grave, so she could have the birds close to her in death as they were throughout her life. A handcrafted round mosaic with the red Burggraf "B" sat in the center of her site, and figure skates were etched into her tombstone. After the committal service, the funeral party headed back to the church where the others waited. "I had never seen such rough and tumble guys show such respect, composure, and emotion," said Lou of the two hockey teams. "Nancy had touched every one of their lives. Even the bus drivers came out and stood with the players and coaches."

Back at the church, Bernie grabbed Lee Goren, outstanding scorer for the Sioux. Lee and teammate Mike Commodore were thinking about turning professional before their senior year at UND.

"Lee," said Bernie. "Nancy saw on TV that you had received an offer from the Bruins. I tell you, she clapped her hands for me to bring her a pad and pencil. It's one of the last things she ever wrote."

Bernie handed Lee the letter.

"Both you and Mike should stay and finish school. Use another year to develop as a player and a person. Then take your ticket to the pros or whatever the case might be. Nancy B."

Both players finished college.

"The matter was decided as soon as Bernie approached me," said Lee, who had scored a team high 26 goals as a junior and had been offered a third-round draft choice by Boston. He would have bolted from college for the right contract.

"I might have left," Lee said. "But with Nancy's letter on my shoulders and in my heart, it didn't matter what they would offer. I was going back to UND."

"Nancy's letter wasn't the entire reason behind my decision," said Mike, "but where there is someone who is nice like that and you respect, you take it all to heart and take it into consideration." The New Jersey managers, who selected Mike in the second-round draft, also had advised him to stay in school.

• • •

Lee Goren and Mike Commodore went on to play their final seasons with the Sioux. They won the National Championship in 2000, and Dean Blais feels the memory of Nancy Burggraf inspired his team to win it all. Lee went on to play with the Boston Bruins and Mike with the New Jersey Devils.

• • •

Nancy received over 100 unsolicited letters nominating her for the United States Hockey Hall of Fame. The nomination process only requires one letter. Selection committee chairman John Mayasich said, to his amazement that the letters "came from former UND players, from amateur hockey people, pro hockey people, and civilians." Nancy's supporters thought she would be the perfect choice for enshrinement because she was no prima donna, nor a business-minded zealot who exploited hockey for financial reward. She was a pure, grass-roots teacher. Dean Blais suggested that after all she had done for hockey, and her tragic illness, timing was important. But in 1999, the Hall of Fame voting process was delayed and took place after Nancy's death.

Sports reporter John Gilbert, a member of the Hall of Fame selection committee said, "None of the eastern [U.S.] voters knew of Nancy's story, and I tried to tell it. Some of the western voters were too far removed from the grassroots to know her compelling story. The chances were slim. She became famous as a skating instructor, but her fame came with reluctance because she never wanted the spotlight. Which is one reason why she deserved it."

In his column, John also wrote that Nancy would have applauded the three selections made that year and would have been embarrassed to be included with them. Nancy remained on the nomination list for three years until 2001 and was then removed from consideration. John wrote that "if the U.S. Hockey Hall of Fame isn't big enough for Nancy Burggraf, then it simply isn't big enough."

"Nancy will always be remembered as a pioneer in the power skating business." —Aaron Broten, former Minnesota North Star

After the burial and back at the church, Bernie told the gathering that Nancy was strong, courageous, and contagious in her faith, without beating a drum or seeking the spotlight.

"She believed," he said, "that actions speak louder than words." He remembered one night sitting with her in the hospital. "She clapped and I got the writing pad. One of her last nights she wrote: 'I want you to be strong.' She was a good teacher, and I am trying very hard to listen."

Notes From Nancy Burggraf's "Stick Down, Head Up!" Training Manual

"Motivation is what gets you started, dedication is what keeps you going, and desire is what gets you there." —Nancy Burggraf

Puck Handling

Carrying the puck while skating takes considerable concentration and practice. "Soft hands" is a term you will hear about players who have developed excellent puck-handling skills. We develop skating skills first before beginning to work with a puck. The puck will distract a skater's concentration away from his skating, and he will concentrate only on the puck, rather than his skating skills or the drills at hand. Consequently, his skating skills will suffer.

It is important to use your peripheral vision and to keep your head up while carrying the puck. This should be taught to younger skaters at the early stages of the game. It is a basic fundamental that often goes uncoached. The more you move the puck, the more you risk losing it. Most players over-handle it. You want to keep the puck flat on the ice at all times, which will offer the best results for control and handling, shooting, and accurate passing.

Be positive with the puck. Keep your feet moving with your head up and communicate with one another on the ice. In any offense, the most important person is not the puck carrier but the other players.

*"Develop the single most important aspect of playing hockey . . .
your individual skating skills." —Nancy Burggraf*

Walk on Ice: Ankle Building Drill

Tiptoe-walking on skates across the ice is an excellent calf and ankle development. For a complete workout stay on the toes at all times. Keep the stick high overhead as you walk. Then begin to increase to a "quick step" on toes.

Work hard and stay with it when the burning sensation starts. When done properly, this drill will improve balance, strength, coordination, and conditioning. Use it to break up practice and implement it for a conditioning "breather" between conditioning drills.

"Kids on ice stay out of hot water." —Nancy Burggraf

Shoot the Duck (also called the "frying pan")

This drill is a "favorite" of all skaters in the Burggraf clinics and schools across the country. Shoot the Duck can be intimidating, and the skater will overflow with excitement once he masters it. The drill will develop balance, flexibility, strength, and confidence. It takes practice for the skater to learn to control the body's weight distribution over the edges.

To begin, obtain speed using the long stride and skating from the hips and down. Once in the glide, assume a squatting position (butt down) with your weight on the flat edges. Keep the body weight slightly forward. Shift weight to the flat edge of one skate and lift the other skate forward, extending it out in front and holding it off the ice. Hold this position as long as you can, "shooting" for the other end of the ice.

Once you have mastered this, rapidly switch feet (Russian) while in the squatting position. Then repeat it going backward.

Butterfly Flicks

The objective of Butterfly Flicks is to improve the goalie's agility, flexibility, quickness, strength, and confidence while down on his pads. The goalie should not be down on his pads much of the time. The best goalie is a stand-up goalie. Because hockey is so fast, there will be times when he needs the ability to quickly "flick" out his pad to make a save.

For the drill, assume a kneeling position on your pads. Keep your stick on the ice in front of you with your back straight and head up. Transfer your weight onto your right pad and "flick" your left leg out to the side, keeping the pad forward. Bend at your waist and lean out over your extended pad as far as you can. Return to the starting position and transfer your weight onto the left pad. Then flick your right leg out. Take your time until you have the technique down and then begin to increase speed. It is a tiring drill; work hard at it.

"Remember to take your time and do the drills right." —Nancy Burggraf

Bibliography

⸛

Chapters 1, 2, and 3

Abram, Terry. Telephone interview. Minneapolis, June 8, 2001.

"Bergetta Harris." Biography loose files, provided by Harris/Burggraf family, document 2034, Roseau County Historical Society. Roseau, circa 1972-73.

City of Roseau. http://city.roseau.mn.us/history/overview.html (accessed June 2001).

"Dr. R.V. Harris recalls early days of dentistry." *Roseau Times Region*. Roseau, 1972.

Gotziaman, Terry. Personal interview with Chris Mohs and Sarah McCurdy. Roseau, February 16, 2001.

"Guide to Roseau County." Supplement to *Roseau Times Region*. Roseau, November 2000.

Harris, Bob. Personal interview. Warroad, July 7, 2002.

Huglen, Erling. "Bergetta Harris will be missed." *Roseau Times Region*. Roseau, December 29, 1995.

"North Star City, Roseau, Minnesota." Roseau Chamber of Commerce. Roseau, 2002.

"Richard Van Sant Harris." Biography loose files, provided by Harris/Burggraf family, document 2033, Roseau County Historical Society. Roseau, circa 1972-73.

"Roseau Profile." www.rrv.net/roseau/profile.html (accessed June 2001).

"Services for Dr. R.V. Harris." *Roseau Times Region*. Roseau, June 25, 1973.

Chapter 4 and 5

Burggraf, Charlie. Personal interview. Minneapolis, Minnesota. June 23, 2001.

Burggraf, Frank. Personal interview. Fargo, North Dakota. July 12, 2001.

Burggraf, Pearl. Letter to Nancy Harris. Stephen, Minnesota. February 1951.

"Candidates for Ice Carnival Queen." *The Concordian*. Concordia College newspaper, Moorhead, February 17, 1950.

"Cobbers Elect Queen." *The Concordian*. Concordia College newspaper. Moorhead, February 27, 1950.

Harris, Sally "Cook". Personal interview. Roseau, June 23, 2001.

Haukebo, Doris. Personal interview by Hannah Dahl. Moorhead, June 5, 2001.

"Homecoming Committee Named." *The Concordian*. Concordia College newspaper, Moorhead, September 29, 1950.

"It's Yea Cobbers, Go Gang Go." *The Concordian*, Concordia College newspaper, Moorhead, September 3, 1949.

Klemer, Dar. Telephone interview by Hannah Dahl. Moorhead, May 29, 2001.

Klemer, Dar. Personal interview by Hannah Dahl. Faribault, October 4, 2001

"More Cobbers Receive Diamonds." *The Concordian*. Concordia College newspaper. Moorhead, February 1951.

"Nancy Jean Harris Weds Bernard Burggraf." *Roseau Times Region*. Roseau, January 10, 1952.

"Pretty Co-eds Lead Cobber Cheers." *The Concordian*. Concordia College newspaper, Moorhead, September 22, 1950.

Rambler, Roseau High School Yearbook. Roseau, 1948.

Shaw, Joseph. M. "Post War Oles." *History of St. Olaf College, 1874-1974*. St. Olaf College Press, Northfield, 1974.

"Seniors of 1952." *Cobber Yearbook*. Concordia College, Moorhead, 1952.

Sorenson, Bergetta. Letter to Bernard Burggraf. Roseau, February 1951.

St. Olaf Stands. St. Olaf College Archives. Northfield, 1947.

Student Handbook. St. Olaf College Archives. Northfield, 1946.

Chapter 6

Burggraf, Charlie. Personal interview. Minneapolis, June 23, 2001.

Burggraf, Frank. Personal interview. Fargo, North Dakota, February 2, 2002.

Burggraf, Rick. Personal interview. Fargo, North Dakota, February 2, 2002.

"Cinderella to be played by skaters." *Roseau Times Region*. Roseau, February 23, 1956.

"Cinderella to be given here." *Roseau Times Region*. Roseau, March 3, 1956.

Houger, Diann. Personal interview. Roseau, Minnesota. January 11, 2002.

"Ice Show Top Attraction." *Roseau Times Region*. Roseau, March 12, 1959.

Lommen, Becky. Personal interview. Moorhead, September 21, 2001.

Marx, Darlyn. Telephone interview by Hannah Dahl. Moorhead, November 17, 2001.

"Sixty-two girls will figure skate." *Roseau Times Region*. Roseau, February 12, 1956.

"Skating Club has 90 girls enrolled now." *Roseau Times Region*. Roseau, February 18, 1956.

"Skating Club sets ice revue." *Roseau Times Region*. Roseau, March 5, 1959.

"Took part in Cinderella." *Roseau Times Region*. Roseau, March 8, 1956.

Chapter 7

Burggraf, Bernie. Personal interview by Chris Mohs and Sarah McCurdy. Roseau, February 12, 2002.

Burggraf, Charlie. Personal interview. Minneapolis, June 22, 2001.

Burggraf, Frank. Personal interview. Fargo, North Dakota. June 23, 2001.

Burggraf, Rick. Personal interview. Fargo, North Dakota. June 22, 2001.

Erickson, Jeremy. Personal interview. Minneapolis, February 7, 2002.

Pederson, Julie. "Burggraf's celebrates 42 years of doing business in Roseau." *Roseau Times Region*. Roseau, September 23, 1994.

Chapter 8

Burggraf, Nancy. *Stick Down Head Up*. Training Manual. Fargo, North Dakota: Killion Communications, 1992.

Baumgartner, Mike. Personal interview. Roseau, June 22, 2001.

Baumgartner, Paul. Personal interview. Roseau, June 22, 2001.

Bjorkman, Rube. Personal interview. Roseau, January 11, 2002.

Boucha, Henry. Personal interview. Warroad, January 11, 2002.

Brandt, Jake. Personal interview. Roseau, July 28, 2001.

Broten, Aaron. Personal interview. Roseau, June 23, 2001.

Carlson, Michael. Personal interview. Moorhead, August 13, 2001.

Larson, Phil. Personal interview. Roseau, July 28, 2001.

Lundbolm, Andy. Personal interview. Roseau, June 23, 2001.

Kraft, Ryan. Personal interview. Moorhead, August 13, 2001.

Olson, Bruce. Personal interview. Roseau, June 23, 2001.

"Power skating classes offered." *Roseau Times Region*. Roseau, August 3, 1978.

"Power skating instructor, Nancy Harris Burggraf." *Roseau Times Region*. Roseau, December 11, 1984.

Strandell, Harold. "White skated instructor turns snickers into power." *Grand Forks Herald*. Grand Forks, North Dakota. April 4, 1976.

Chapter 9

Coleman, Nick. "Hockey is life." *St. Paul Pioneer Press*. St. Paul, January 31, 1999.

Roseau vs. Warroad Hockey Game. Roseau, January 2002.

Chapter 10

Baumgartner, Steve. Personal interview. Roseau, January 22, 2002.

Berry, Nathan. Personal interview. Roseau, August 13, 2001.

Bjorkman, Rube. Personal interview. Roseau, January 11, 2002.

Blais, Dean. Personal interview by Chris Mohs and Sarah McCurdy. Grand Forks, North Dakota, February 6, 2002.

Burggraf, Frank. Personal interview. Moorhead, February 12, 2002.

Burggraf, Sally (Cook). Personal interview. Roseau, October 13, 2001.

Eades, Carey. Personal interview. Roseau, June 23, 2001.

Kraft, Ryan. Personal interview. Moorhead, August 13, 2001.

Mertz, Adam. "Sioux's inspiration a first class lady." *Capital Times*. Madison, Wisconsin. January 14, 2000.

Meyer, Jess. "Lady in figure skates became authoritative hockey teacher." Minnesota State High School Hockey League Tournament Book. Minneapolis, 1999.

Sandlin, Scott. Personal interview. Roseau, June 23, 2001.

Chapter 11

Burggraf, Bernie. Personal interview. Roseau, February 12, 2002.

Burggraf, Charlie. Personal interview. Minneapolis, February 20, 2002.

Burggraf, Nancy. Personal journals. Roseau, 1987–1996.

Hermansen, Lou. Personal interview. Roseau, January 11, 2002.

Johnson, Eleanor. Personal interview. Roseau, June 23, 2001.

Proznik, Bill. "Burggraf makes hefty contributions to game of hockey." *Pioneer Press*. St. Paul, October 19, 1973.

Chapter 12

Burggraf, Bernie. Personal interview. Roseau, February 12, 2002.

Burggraf, Nancy. Personal journals. Roseau, 1996–1997.

Lommen, Mike. "My Nana," via e-mail. Moorhead, October 10, 2001.

Chapter 13

"ALS immobilizes hockey skating guru." *Grand Fork Herald*. Grand Forks, North Dakota, November 2, 1998.

Burggraf, Nancy. Personal journals. Roseau, 1997–1999.

"Burggraf's closes its doors after 46 years." *Roseau Times Region*. Roseau, January 19, 1999.

Foss, Steve. "Longtime Roseau mayor declines re-election bid." *Grand Forks Herald*. Grand Forks, North Dakota. October 31, 1998.

Foss, Steve. "Stick down head Up." *Grand Forks Herald*. Grand Forks, North Dakota, November 2, 1998.

Haga, Chuck. "Now limited by disease, skating coach helped many reach NHL." *Minneapolis Star Tribune*. Minneapolis, November 16, 1998.

Huglen, Erling. "Burggraf drops out of mayor's race." *Roseau Times Region*. Roseau, October 31, 1998.

"Lifetime hockey teacher diagnosed with Gehrig's Disease." *The Forum of Fargo Moorhead*. Fargo, North Dakota, November 2, 1998.

Chapter 14 and 15

Augustouz, Roman. "Roseau roars to title." *Star Tribune*. Minneapolis, March 7, 1999.

Brandt, Jake. Personal interview. Roseau, July 28, 2001.

Burggraf, Bernie. Personal interview. Roseau, February 12, 2002.

Burggraf, Sally (Cook). Personal interview by Chris Mohs and Sarah McCurdy. Roseau, October 13, 2001.

Olson, Bruce. Personal interview. Roseau, June 23, 2001.

Fee, Kevin. "Rams hold true to promise made to Nancy Burggraf." *Grand Forks Herald*. Grand Forks, North Dakota, April 11, 1999.

Gilbert, John. "Roseau aims to win one for old time's sake." *Up North Newspaper Network*. Duluth, March 3, 1999.

Gilbert, John. "State title more than hockey to Roseau." *Up North Newspaper Network*. Duluth, March 10, 1999.

Gotziaman, Terry. Personal interview by Chris Mohs and Sarah McCurdy. Roseau, February 16, 2001.

"Minnesota State Hockey Finals: Roseau vs. Hastings." KMSP Television. Minneapolis, March 6, 1999.

Larson, Phil. Personal interview. Roseau, July 28, 2001.

"Rams dedicate tourney to Burggraf." *Grand Forks Herald*. Grand Forks, North Dakota, March 4, 1999.

"Roseau begins AA title drive." *Star Tribune*. Minneapolis, March 4, 1999.

"State Hockey Tournament Supplement." *Roseau Times Region*. Roseau, March 10, 1999.

Chapter 16 and 17

Burggraf, Bernie. Personal interview. Roseau, February 12, 2002.

Burggraf, Sally (Cook). Personal interview. Roseau, October 13, 2001.

Dennis, Tom. "Burggraf set an inspiring example." *Grand Forks Herald*. Grand Forks, North Dakota, April 6, 1999.

Erickson, Jeremy. Personal interview. Minneapolis, January 19, 2002.

Erickson, Jeremy. Personal interview. Minneapolis, February 7, 2002.

Foss, Steve. "Roseau loses a community leader." *Grand Forks Herald*. Grand Forks, North Dakota, April 6, 1999.

Haga, Chuck. "Nancy Burggraf dies; taught skating skills to future NHL stars." *Star Tribune*. Minneapolis, April 6, 1999.

Lommen, Becky. Personal interview. Moorhead, September 21, 2001.

Spina, Meghan. Senior English composition Roseau High School. Roseau, Spring 2000.

Chapter 18

Blais, Dean. Personal interview with Chris Mohs and Sarah McCurdy. Grand Forks, North Dakota, February 6, 2002.

Burggraf, Bernie. Personal interview. Roseau, February 12, 2002.

Burggraf, Rick. Personal interview. Fargo, North Dakota, February 6, 2002.

Dunavan, Naomi. "Roseau residents, UND hockey players bid farewell to NancyBurggraf." *Grand Forks Herald*. Grand Forks, North Dakota, April 10, 1999.

Fee, Kevin. "Goren gives father a nice birthday gift." *Grand Forks Herald*. Grand Forks, North Dakota, April 9, 2000.

Foss, Steve. "Roseau loses a community leader." *Grand Forks Herald*. Grand Forks, North Dakota, April 6, 1999.

Foss, Virg. "Goren to return for final season." *Grand Forks Herald*. Grand Forks, North Dakota, April 16, 1999.

Gilbert, John. "Nancy Burggraf would be perfect Hockey Hall of Fame inductee." *Roseau Times Region*. Roseau, December 11, 1999.

Hermansen, Lou. Personal interview. Roseau, January 11, 2002.

Houger, Diann. Personal interview. Roseau, January 11, 2002.

Huglen, Erling. "Easter and hockey—two of Nancy's favorite things." *Roseau Times Region*. Roseau, April 10, 1999.

Mertz, Adam. "Sioux's inspiration a first-class lady." *Capital Times*. Madison, Wisconsin, January 14, 2000.

"Nancy Burggraf Funeral Service." Messiah Lutheran Church. Roseau, April 9, 1999.

"Roseau bids farewell to a true champion." *Roseau Times Region*. Roseau, April 10, 1999.

About the Author

Merrie Sue Holtan

Merrie Sue Holtan teaches communication studies at Minnesota State University–Moorhead. A native of Rushford, Minnesota, she has an undergraduate degree from the University of Minnesota and master's degrees in communication and writing from North Dakota State University and MSUM.

She has been a freelance writer for more than 20 years and is interested in documenting "stories gone missing." She also serves as managing editor of OPEN magazine, the city and lifestyle magazine of Fargo-Moorhead.

Her other publications include: *Y Winners: Cookbook of Championships*, a cookbook for young athletes, and *Sink or Swim? Best Practices in Advising for Vocation*, for college academic advisers.

Merrie Sue and her husband, Rev. Phil Holtan, live on Big Pine Lake near Perham, Minnesota. They have three grown children.